TWELVE
LIES
YOU HEAR IN
CHURCH

TWELVE LIES YOU HEAR IN CHURCH

Tim Riter

Building the New Generation of Believers

An Imprint of Cook Communications Ministries • Colorado Springs, CO

NexGen is an imprint of
Cook Communications Ministries, Colorado Springs, CO 80918
Cook Communications, Paris, Ontario
Kingsway Communications, Eastbourne, England

TWELVE LIES YOU HEAR IN CHURCH
© 2004 by TIM RITER

www.timriter.com

First Printing, 2004
Printed in the United States of America
1 2 3 4 5 6 7 Printing/Year 08 07 06 05 04

Library of Congress Cataloging-in-Publication Data

Riter, Tim, 1948-
  Twelve lies you hear in church / by Tim Riter.
     p. cm.
  ISBN 0-7814-4005-X
  1. Christian life. 2. Theology, Doctrinal–Popular works. I. Title.
  BV4501.3.R58 2004
  248.4–dc21

                                    2003004658

Many years ago, a pastor and his wife
took a chance on a fairly young minister.
The young guy discovered their eagerness
for the truth, their dedication to stand up for it,
and their willingness to pay a price
for confronting untruth.
He learned much from them.
Herb and Thelma Read,
thank you for those lessons.
This one's for you!

Contents

Introduction

Trapped by the Lie

You can't really love the truth
'til you've been trapped by the lie.
—John Fischer

I've spent most of my life in church. I practically grew up there, accepting Christ at age eleven and committing myself to the ministry shortly thereafter. I sincerely, but superficially, tried to do what was right, seeking to please God by pleasing others. It wasn't long, though, before I learned that doing what others told me I "should" wouldn't build a faith that could withstand the tests of life.

As a young adult, I embarked on several years of healthy searching and discovered the solid historical and logical foundations of Christianity. Though I hadn't yet returned to my walk with God, I teetered on the edge of commitment.

Even during this time of searching, I still tried to do what was right, what I thought Christians were supposed to do—mostly, anyway. I struggled particularly with a deeply ingrained self-centeredness—wanting to be a more giving person, wanting to look out for the needs of others—but with no success. That failure shattered my self-confidence. Most goals I deeply desired I'd been able to attain, but not this one.

Finally, I turned to God. "God, if you're real—and I think you are—I yield my life to you. I give you full freedom to change me. Lord, I want to get beyond doing everything for myself. Do whatever you want to make me who you want me to be."

He did. Almost overnight, my priorities changed. Something beyond me transformed who I was. My desire to be selfless began to become reality, and it was accompanied by a power I'd never experienced. I'd worked very hard to change my self-centered nature and failed. I knew this new person I was becoming could only be a result of God's power at work in my life.

That Was Then

With the change came relaxation. I'd surrendered. I'd arrived. I was spiritual. Other aspects of my life seemed pretty decent, so I was certain I could enjoy the Christian ride from here on out.

As that attitude took hold of my life, I got trapped by one of Satan's lies. I quit growing, mistakenly believing I could stay in spiritual kindergarten. I was happy using paste and crayons and had no desire to move toward markers and glue sticks! I thought I'd worked enough.

Because I really enjoyed my contented feelings, some time passed before I realized those feelings didn't come from God. Buying into the lie slowed me down for a while. Once I learned the danger of that untruth, however, I got back on track and grew spiritually.

This Is Now

In over twenty years of pastoring, I've identified several misconceptions that keep sincere believers from growing in Christ. At our local pastors' fellowship, someone asked about my latest book idea. My response, *Twelve Lies You Hear in Church*, prompted more laughter than I expected and a sly comment from one of my colleagues: "Tim, how can you keep it at just twelve?"

I'm convinced most Christians want God's best, but we can't receive what we don't even know we need! Many of our assumptions and beliefs about faith deceive us and keep us from growing. Lies and half-truths pack tremendous power to damage us. I learned that the hard way.

Sources of Lies

We can pick up false ideas in a multitude of ways: a well-intentioned but ignorant teacher, a leader with a personal agenda, an unspoken yet clearly communicated attitude within a church, assumptions we make ourselves. Sometimes we hear these distortions explicitly; sometimes we just absorb them like radio waves. Whatever their source, they abound, and we buy into them more often than we think.

DON'T KNOW

Sometimes we accept a lie because we've never been taught the truth, and we just don't have the correct knowledge. Maybe our teachers believe the lie—for whatever reason—so we're not exposed to the truth.

DON'T CARE

Other times we accept the lie because it matches what we want to believe. We actually prefer the lie. Maybe there's a behavior or habit we don't want to give up, so we argue against the truth. Maybe we're unwilling to forgive, so we focus on "an eye for an eye" and neglect "love your enemies." Maybe the concept of change itself makes us uncomfortable, so we accept Jesus as Savior but not as Lord.

When we've been exposed to truth but resist it, we stay stuck in a lie. But what happens when we look for truth and don't receive it, even from the place we most expect to find it?

MISLED BY THE CHURCH

I love the church. I've spent most of my life in it, and I've given my life to serving it. But sometimes we in the church can subtly provide false messages. For instance, we can focus so much on attendance and giving that we fear calling people to a higher standard of discipleship. And when we do that, we unknowingly pass on a lie.

The elders of a southern California church reviewed candidates for new elders, and they got stuck on Larry. Involved in the church from the early days, he had a true servant's heart. He made himself available for anything from sweeping the sidewalk to teaching Sunday school. Something was missing, though. Larry never demonstrated a deep love of God. He didn't join any of the midweek Bible studies or make any apparent effort to grow in his faith. Although a nice guy, he didn't exhibit a great deal of character change, he just kept "doing."

Then someone nominated him for elder. The elders reviewed his qualifications, but Larry just didn't seem like elder material. Frank spoke up. "You know, Larry has a lot of pride, and he knows he was nominated. I'm afraid if we turn him down, he may leave the church. His kids make up the core of the youth group, and he's a generous giver. Let's not cause any trouble; just put him on the ballot."

Frank convinced the others, but in the process, what did the church teach? "We care most about 'nickels and noses.' You don't have to grow in spiritual maturity. We care more about your attendance than your spiritual well being."

Too many members hear the church whisper, "You can stay in kindergarten. We'll accept that. And if we do, God must do the same thing."

Whatever the source, any misconception can easily side-track or slow down our spiritual walk. But as we discover biblical truth, we free ourselves to become all that God designed us to be and to "walk at his pace." Although untruth possesses power, truth inherently provides more.

The Power of the Truth

As we ask the Holy Spirit to reveal our misconceptions, we remove roadblocks to our spiritual journey. That's the message of Jesus in John 8:32: "Then you will *know the truth,* and the truth *will set you free"* (emphasis added).

Knowing the truth yields the best God has to offer. The truth reveals chains that bind us. The truth reveals the correct path to follow. The truth furnishes insights into the attractiveness of knowing God deeply. The truth tells us areas where we need to mature. Only when we know and accept the truth can we cooperate with Jesus and grow.

So, how do we gain the spiritual freedom Jesus talked about? By a quest for the truth. We ruthlessly examine our lives, our beliefs, our attitudes, and our assumptions to see if untruth has crept into our thinking or behavior. If it has, we must seek out God's truth and allow his Holy Spirit to change our minds and actions.

That's what this book is about: helping you to uncover the lies, to recognize the truth, and to experience the freedom God has waiting for you. Remember the response from my pastor friend? He was right. We certainly have more than twelve misconceptions out there. For that reason, I'll also give you some tools you can use to identify other untruths that may be stunting your spiritual growth. As we uncover these twelve lies we hear in church, as we discover the corresponding truth, and as we learn to apply the principles in other areas of our lives, we'll all be free to know God as he wants us to know him. Welcome to the adventure!

Log the Truth

1. If you had to classify your spiritual walk in terms of human development, where would you fit? (Newborn? Adolescent? Retired? Unborn? Middle-aged?)

2. What is the most apparent misconception you have encountered?

3. In what ways did it slow down your spiritual growth?

4. What is the most obvious source of lies in your life?

Lie 1

I Believe in Jesus and That's Enough

The Truth about Saving Faith

Brian seemed to have everything going for him. He'd been transferred to our town with a great promotion and was looking for a church home. One of our members, Nick, worked with him and invited him to play basketball with our church team. He soon got deeply involved.

He'd been a Christian for nearly his entire life and fit right in with us. He spoke often of how much he loved God and appreciated his presence. He became a regular participant in one of our home groups, where grace was a favorite subject of his. Almost too much of a favorite.

When discussions touched salvation, Brian strongly emphasized that we're saved by faith alone without doing anything. He became known for that, but he wasn't pushy. Just determined. I never dreamed how determined.

A few months later, Nick approached me. "Pastor, I'm concerned about Brian. I don't know an easy way to say this, but he's carrying on an affair with one of the married women at work. All the employees know it, and they know he's a Christian and that he goes to our church. I don't want to judge him, but he's hurting the Lord's reputation, and I know he's skating on thin ice. I just think we've got to do something, at least check it out. Can you talk to him?"

The joys of pastoring! I made a lunch appointment with Brian and told him I'd heard that something might be going on with a coworker, but I wanted to get the straight scoop from him. Without any hesitation, he confirmed it.

"Pastor, Jeanne and I are both adults. We know what we're doing. Her marriage is emotionally dead, and I'm able to give her some affection. No one's getting hurt since they don't have any kids. The bottom line is it's none of your business. We're going to continue."

"Brian, I'm most concerned about how you can carry on a sexual relationship with a married woman, not be bothered by that, and claim to be a Christian. Those behaviors don't go well together."

"Says who? I've always been taught we're saved by faith alone, not by anything we do. Jesus paid for my sins on the cross; I don't have to. Do *you* remember Ephesians 2:8–9? It says salvation isn't by our works. If I'm saved by faith, not works, then I live by faith, not works.

"Faith is what I believe, not what I do. Didn't you preach recently that the Greek words for faith and belief are the same? I believe Jesus is my Savior; that means I have saving faith. What I do has little relevance to that."

The conversation was fruitless. Brian bought into the lie that saving faith merely is a verbal confession of Jesus as Savior. That lie brought tremendous spiritual damage to him. The last time I talked to him, little had changed. He continued to live just as he pleased, while still claiming allegiance to Christ. And he found a church that let him live as he desired.

What lie did Brian fall prey to? Faith is what we believe, not what we do. Whether expressed in continuing sin or by a lack of growth, those who believe this lie miss the truth that faith is transformation.

Identify the Lie

At least in practice, many Christians believe the lie that faith doesn't involve transformation. Just accepting Christ is acceptably within God's will. We have no need to continue to change and grow.

If we didn't buy into that lie, then why is the divorce rate for Christians so close to that of unbelievers? Why have ninety percent of Christians never led a person to saving faith? Why do ten to twenty percent of church members do ninety percent of the church work? Why do so many studies indicate the behavior of Christians is not that different from unbelievers?

That same lie afflicted the Christians in the first-century city of Corinth. The apostle Paul identified three categories of Christians in chapter three of his first letter to that church. Two of them are acceptable; one twists the truth.

Verses 1–3 read, "Brothers, I could not address you as *spiritual* but as *worldly*—mere infants in Christ. I gave you milk, not solid food, for you were not yet ready for it. Indeed, you are still not ready. You are still *worldly*" (emphasis added).

Let's follow Paul's process of describing the Christian life. We all begin as infants in Christ. That's normal. Just as human infants learn through our mistakes, just as we make some messes, just as we use milk for food, so do spiritual babies. We don't expect an infant to run the New York City Marathon nor eat a New York steak. We don't expect a new Christian to be able to teach clearly on the Trinity.

That's the meaning of the first word Paul used for "worldly," *sarkinos,* in verse one. Not at all negative, this just refers to being made of flesh and influenced by our physical nature. We begin here.

The goal is to be transformed into being "spiritual," as Paul wished in verse one. Spiritual Christians have grown beyond the baby stage. The Holy Spirit plays a greater role in their daily lives and decision-making. Observers can easily see the influence of the Spirit on their lives. Spiritual Christians aren't perfect, but they are making progress.

However, some Christians stay in spiritual kindergarten. They should be in high school but haven't yet learned to read. This is the perversion, a major departure from the progression of the Christian life. Paul uses a slightly different "worldly" to describe them in verse three. The word is *sarkikos,* a subtle but significant change.

Sarkikos refers to the flesh dominating. When our old desires, which we should have learned how to handle, still handle us, we continue in our old sins. Our fleshly nature appears stronger than our spiritual one. We don't grow beyond being an infant in Christ. We've bought into the lie that Christians have no need to change.

How can we tell if we're stunted in our transformation? Throughout 1 Corinthians, Paul describes the non-transformed Christian life. One trait is found in the remainder of verse three: "For since there is jealousy and quarreling among you, are you not *worldly [sarkikos]?* Are you not acting like *mere men?*" (emphasis added).

"Mere men" are people who function without the primary influence of the Spirit. Still quarreling, too much like they used to be.

Paul adds to this list of worldliness with traits like disunity (1:10-13), sexual immorality (5:1-13; 6:9-20), lawsuits among believers (6:1-8), marriage and divorce problems (7:1-40), abuse of Christian freedom (8:1-13), disorderly worship services (11:1-34), abuse of spiritual gifts (chapters 12-14), and an incorrect focus on the Second Coming (15:1-58).

Sounds like current history, doesn't it? Maybe we, too, are afflicted with the lie that transformation isn't a vital part of faith. Where do we get such an idea? Two factors lead us into the lie.

MISUNDERSTANDING SAVING FAITH

Misunderstanding biblical faith can be dangerous. The Bible clearly states we're saved by faith alone, but not by a faith that *is* alone. We sometimes theorize that since we can't do anything to get saved, our actions mean nothing spiritually.

Ephesians 2:8-9 affirms the first part of that theory: "For it is by grace you have been saved, through faith—and this not from yourselves, it is the gift of God—not by works, so that no one can boast." That's clear. We do nothing to gain salvation. But the second part of that theory is destroyed by verse 10: "For we are God's workmanship, *created in Christ Jesus to do good works,* which God prepared in advance for us *to do"* (emphasis added).

Works play a major role in the Christian life. Not before salvation, to earn it, but after. That's our transformation— becoming spiritual—moving beyond those traits Paul mentioned in 1 Corinthians.

This lie can bring tremendous damage to our lives when we embrace it by thinking behavior has nothing to do with our faith. We counter this lie by knowing that saving faith includes changing our behavior after we come to Christ.

Misunderstanding Growth

The entire Bible excites me, but some passages intrigue me more than others. Second Corinthians 5:17 fits that latter category: "Therefore, if anyone is in Christ, he is a *new creation*; the old has gone, the new has come!" (emphasis added).

What does Paul mean when he says we become a new person? When I committed my life to Christ, my name stayed the same; my face and body did also. I didn't need a new driver's license photo, although I wouldn't have minded one! But two revolutionary changes occurred. First, my spirit was made new. I was able to connect with God. I began to know him.

Second, my values and behavior began to change. Some were instant and dramatic; others took longer and were subtle. Do you remember Paul's description of three levels of faith from 1 Corinthians 3? God wants us to begin as immature spiritual babies and to grow into spiritually mature adults.

God loves us just as we are, but he also loves us too much to leave us as we are. When we miss out on this truth, we fall prey to the lie that spiritual growth is an option rather than a privilege.

Learn the Truth

Do you remember my story at the beginning of the book? When God made the great change in me? I thought I'd arrived, but God loved me too much to leave me there. I was willing to grow; I just thought we'd done enough!

Gently God whispered, "Tim, I'm real proud of what you've allowed me to do, but are you aware that we need to work on another area?"

I said I wasn't, and he promptly told me which one. Not surprisingly, he was right, but I'd never thought of that part of my life as a topic he'd be concerned with. Once again we worked together, more changes were made, and again, I wanted to relax.

God had other ideas and whispered once more, "Tim, I'm pleased, but have you thought about ...?" By now I knew the drill. And I was starting to learn the lesson: God wants to transform us.

We overcome the lie when we grasp the truth that God offers us transformation as part of the salvation package. We have the privilege of growing beyond our old weaknesses. God wouldn't love us if he allowed our old problems to continue. The essence of faith is a relationship where we value knowing God above all. Such a relationship makes us willing to change our lives to better know him.

CHRISTIANITY IS TRANSFORMATION

The truth about saving faith is found in the word *transformation*. Look at Romans 12:2: "Do not conform any longer to the pattern of this world, but *be transformed* by the renewing of your mind. Then you will be able to test and approve what God's will is—his good, pleasing, and perfect will" (emphasis added).

Notice again that the end gives the goal: God's good will for us. What is that? That we be transformed. That word *transformed*, in the original language, is our root for *metamorphosis*. That's the process by which a caterpillar changes into a butterfly, the type of change God desires for us.

Transformed is found again in 2 Corinthians 3:18: "And we, who with unveiled faces all reflect the Lord's glory, are *being transformed into his likeness* with ever-increasing glory, which comes from the Lord, who is the Spirit" (emphasis added).

What an awesome privilege! We grow into the likeness of Jesus Christ himself. The glory of God lives within us. The more we reflect that, the more we're changed. We take on Jesus' character. We imitate his behavior. We share his values. We help carry out his mission.

That's the truth. Not only *should* we grow spiritually, we *can* grow spiritually. God gives us that privilege. We become a new person.

Partnering with God for Transformation

Anytime we're involved with God we have a tremendous privilege. Salvation is our first benefit as we experience God's love and grace. That salvation is God's work; we receive it by faith, not by being good. Our role is to just believe.

God, however, desires to establish a working partnership that transforms our lives. If receiving God's salvation is a privilege, then what word would best describe the opportunity to become a partner with the Creator of the universe? God wants to *cooperate* with us in bringing transformation. To reach the goal, both of us need to be involved.

Philippians 2:12–13 provides a fascinating insight into that partnership: "Therefore, my dear friends, as you have always obeyed—not only in my presence, but now much more in my absence—*continue to work out your salvation* with fear and trembling, for it is *God who works in you* to will and to act according to *his good purpose*" (emphasis added).

Let's start at the end: God has a good purpose for your life. As God, he knows best. What method has God chosen to accomplish his goal? A working partnership, a joint venture combining our efforts and God's, to reach our best.

We work out our salvation. The working doesn't *bring* salvation, rather it *extends* salvation to each nook and cranny of our lives. Just like God did with my life after I made the initial commitment. We cooperate with God in spiritual growth.

As a part of that process, God works in us. He provides the power we lack and the forgiveness we crave. He furnishes the grace to grow.

He wouldn't face our resistance, our self-will, and our fleshly weakness. Just like he created the world, God could create godliness in us by speaking a command. I'm impressed that God chose what is by far the most difficult method. Far easier to say, "Grow!" and watch it happen. But he chose a working partnership. We work side by side with God to create a new person, and that's a privilege.

So where are we? We've seen the truth that God wants us to change. We've seen the truth that God partners with us. We next need to understand the truth of how we grow spiritually.

Live the Truth

Growth is normal, and it's a cycle. Rick Warren of Saddleback Valley Community Church presents a clear and simple summary of the process of growth:

Healthy things grow.

Growing things change.

Changing things challenge us.

Challenges make us trust in God.

Trust leads to obedience.

Obedience leads to health.

Healthy things grow.

Once we understand the process, we need to nurture it. We grow physically as we eat wisely and exercise, and the same process applies to spiritual growth.

While books abound on the topic of spiritual growth, don't run to the bookstore just yet. First, immerse yourself in the Word of God, the Bible. Search it to learn God's heart. Also, be involved in a local church and take advantage of its educational opportunities.

Listen to good teachers on the radio, TV, and tapes. Be discerning, though. Place primary importance on your own personal reading, study, memorization, and meditation.

Then exercise. Spiritually, that means to obey commands in the Bible. Don't fall into the trap of disobedience the way Brian did. Discover areas you need to grow in and focus on them. Be involved in ministry on a variety of levels. One of our members began his ministry picking up senior citizens at a nearby retirement home. He now teaches a Sunday school class and leads a home group.

As we combine eating with exercise, we develop a muscular Christianity. We grow far beyond where we started, and gradually, we become transformed into the likeness of Christ.

I still vividly remember those early days as God made clear to me a few changes we needed to make. I thought a few would be enough, but he's still pointing out more. Some he brings to my attention are areas I was proud of just a short time ago. But I hear his voice and want his best for me.

I'm not the same person I was thirty years ago. And if I make another thirty, I hope I won't be the person I am today. God graces us with the privilege to grow beyond our old problems. And that's the truth.

Log the Truth

1. Have you believed that faith is merely what we believe?

2. If so, how has this belief damaged or slowed your walk with God?

3. If not, how has God molded your behavior to reflect your faith?

4. How have your values changed to reflect your status as a new person in Christ?

5. What step will you take to partner with God in your ongoing transformation?

Lie 2

We Must Be Perfect
The Truth about Our Sin Nature

In a classic study, researchers placed pike fish in a tank along with its typical feeder fish. However, the pike swam side by side next to its normal dinner and eventually starved. Why? Just before, the pike was on one side of the tank; the feeder fish swam on the other, separated by a barrier of clear glass. The pike would make a run for its dinner, hit the glass, and the feeder would escape untouched.

That occurred often enough to teach the pike that the feeder fish were untouchables. So, when researchers removed the barrier, the feeder fish were safe. Faced with an unachievable goal, the pike lost hope. The principle: we give up on unattainable goals.

Has that happened to you in your spiritual life? Has your target of a holy life been frustrated so much by failure that you've given up hope? Have you yielded to a life of spiritual mediocrity because spiritual excellence seems beyond your grasp?

Maybe you've fought a particular sin and lost too frequently for comfort. Maybe you've been working on transforming a bad habit and don't see any progress. Or you get frustrated at other Christians who don't live the kind of Christian life they should.

You wonder about the reality of their faith. You sometimes feel like you're one of the few Christians who really "gets it."

You know what the Bible says Christians should do in an area, but you just can't quite live up to it. Or others don't. And, like the pike, you grow discouraged. You like the concept of the Christian life, but it seems unlivable. Good in theory, impossible in practice.

If that describes you, then maybe you've been trapped by another lie, a lie that has enough truth to be attractive and enough falsehood to be deadly.

Identify the Lie

What lie extinguishes hope? The lie that God requires perfect behavior from his people.

We often call that perfectionism, the idea that believers not only can but should live perfect lives. You've seen that a lot, haven't you? But we usually phrase it differently: "If Harold were a real Christian, he wouldn't smoke." But maybe that's too easy. How about, "How can a true Christian vote for a Democrat? You know, that party supports abortion rights." We can get even more specific: "If Sally really meant it, she'd stop gossiping." Or cheating on her taxes. Or her husband, or … and we can continue to fill in the blanks.

Now let's flip it. If *we* were real Christians, we'd get some victory over that sin. We'd have consistent joy instead of the waves of depression that keep coming at us. If *we* truly lived our faith, we'd tithe, or teach junior high boys, or … . Again, we can fill in the blanks.

What's the principle behind these attitudes? That God has behavioral standards. That the Ten Commandments aren't ten "suggestions." That obedience is an essential part of the Christian life. That followers of Jesus should do what Jesus told them to do.

THE TRUTH WITHIN THE LIE

Remember, each lie has some truth, and this one is filled with it. From John 15:10 let's start with how Jesus views the issue: "If you *obey my commands*, you will remain in my love, just as I have obeyed my Father's commands and remain in his love" (emphasis added).

Jesus says that the goal is a love relationship with him. I like that! But what is the condition to that relationship? Obeying what Jesus commanded. Not suggested, but commanded. So at the center of faith is obedience to the commands of Jesus.

Let's continue and see if his core apostles learned that message. In 1 Peter 1:15–16, Peter gives a startling command, one that later we'll see he himself didn't follow completely. But writing under the inspiration of the Holy Spirit he says, "But just as he who called you is holy, so *be holy in all you do*; for it is written: 'Be holy, because I am holy'" (emphasis added).

In the middle is the key phrase, "be holy in all you do." The original language has "be holy" as a command, not a suggestion. God wants holiness from his people. Holiness means to be set apart, to give our lives to God to use as he desires. Certainly included in that is avoiding sin.

We find even less wiggle room with those words "in all you do." Holiness should be seen in all our behavior. By extension, we won't miss the mark to say that God wants us to consistently be used by him and to avoid sin.

Why must we be holy? First, because he commanded it, which is sufficient reason by itself. Second, because he himself is holy. We are to imitate the character of God, and holiness forms its core. Children become like their parents, and we're to become like our heavenly Father. Not to become God, but to express his holy character in all we do.

The loss of wiggle room grows when we discover why another apostle, John, wrote the first of his letters. Very plainly he provides his purpose in 2:1: "My dear children, I write this to you so that *you will not sin*" (emphasis added).

Pretty clear, isn't it? Why would John write to tell us to do something that's impossible? That would be a waste of time, paper, and ink. Apparently, John believed we have the capacity to not sin. Remember, the Holy Spirit guided him here.

Now, let's follow the trail of logic and learn how we can successfully avoid all sin. Yet another apostle, Paul, provides that procedure in 1 Corinthians 10:13:"No temptation has seized you except what is common to man. And God is faithful; he will not let you be tempted beyond what you can bear. But when you are tempted, he will also provide a way out so that you can stand up under it."

Just about every excuse I've ever used to rationalize why I sin is wiped out in that verse. First, my temptations aren't any stronger than yours. Do you tell yourself that? "Yes, Bill's a solid Christian, but he didn't have the bad example of a father that I did. That's why he does better with his kids."

Second, God controls the severity of the temptation. Either it's something we can handle with our current level of spiritual strength, or God has an escape hatch waiting. Either we can handle it, or we can run!

Now, let's look back at where we've been. First, God commands holiness for each of his people. Second, the Bible provides the tools we need to not sin. Third, God controls temptation so that we're never overwhelmed.

That almost sounds ironclad, doesn't it? Perfectionism may be alive and well on the pages of the New Testament. And when we buy into that lie, we reap pain. We reap a sense of failure when we can't consistently conquer a sin. We face discouragement when we give it our best shot and still fall short.

We become judgmental toward other Christians who don't match biblical standards of behavior. A critical spirit seems to drive us when we evaluate others.

And, like the pike, we're tempted to give up. We just can't live this life. Others don't live it. We lose the hope for victory. The standards that the Bible requires of us just can't be lived. We see the command to resist sin. We try, but we fail. We still sin. We fail God.

Or do we? At least, do we fail him in the way we think we do? So far we've seen only one side of this issue, and the Bible covers it all. In no way do I wish to minimize the commands God gives in his Word. Nor do I wish to diminish the essential role that obedience has in the Christian life. (That will become very clear in the next chapter, so don't think I'm a heretic quite yet!)

I do, however, want to emphasize the balance that allows us to see tremendous importance of purity without becoming too discouraged at our inability to live it out. Let's look at that.

Learn the Truth

Yes, without any doubt God commands obedience, that we avoid sin. We just can't get around that. Nor can we get around the reality that we still fail. How can we bring the two together? By recognizing the difference between perfection and progress, between the target and reality. Biblical reality teaches that every believer in God has sinned. Will sin. Always has. Always will. Go back to the context of 1 John. John wrote so that we wouldn't sin. But in 1:8–2:1 he lets us know the rest of the story.

> If we *claim to be without sin*, we deceive ourselves and the truth is not in us. If we confess our sins, he is faithful and just and will forgive us our sins and purify us from all unrighteousness. If we *claim we have not sinned*, we make him out to be a liar and his word has no place in our lives. My dear children, I write this to you so that you will not sin. But if anybody does sin, we have one who speaks to the Father in our defense— Jesus Christ, the Righteous One (emphasis added).

Doesn't verse one sound familiar, where John gave the reason he wrote the letter—so we could avoid sin? But he also knows we won't always. In fact, if we claim to not sin, we sin by lying! Twice in those four verses he emphasizes that Christians will sin. He provides a remedy but acknowledges the reality.

Grab onto that. As a general principle from Scripture, Christians will not always do the proper Christian act. Yet, they're still believers. Should Christians sin? Absolutely not. Do Christians sin? Absolutely yes.

Not only does John give the principle, the entire Bible provides the evidence for that. Read through Genesis. The first people, Adam and Eve, experienced great intimacy with God. And, with only one sin they could do, they did it. Their children followed that example; their oldest son killed his younger brother. Before too much time passed, people became so sinful God decided to destroy the world with a flood. The one exception: righteous Noah and his family. The world's first shipwright then celebrated his survival by getting drunk.

Trace the history of Abraham, "the righteous man of faith." The profile of his spiritual ups and downs looks like a jagged mountain range. To avert a potential threat to his life, he risked causing his wife to commit adultery by telling a king that she was just his sister. Did he acknowledge his sin and turn away from it? No, he did that same thing again years later.

The first king of Israel sought a forbidden séance with a dead prophet. His immediate successor committed adultery and killed the woman's husband to hide her pregnancy. These sin stories fill the Old Testament and continue into the New. The primary apostle, Peter, denied Jesus even after being told he would do so just a few hours earlier. Later he compromised an important principle in order to be accepted. Paul, the architect of the first-century church, called himself the chief of sinners. (A man who once dedicated his life to killing Christians would seem to qualify for that title.)

So, where's the perfectionism? We've seen God's key leaders all fail to fully obey. They shrink back from righteousness; they sin. What makes us think we'd be different? Particularly when God tells us we'll do the same things!

What is the truth that balances our need to obey? The truth that God knows we will sin. Webbed deep within us is the desire, yearning, and inclination to sin. But when we come to Christ, we establish a new spiritual life.

UNDERSTAND OUR DUALITY

We all possess a strange, almost contradictory, combination of sin and spirit. Listen to how Paul described that duality (Galatians 5:16–17): "So I say, live by the Spirit, and you will not gratify the desires of the sinful nature. For the sinful nature desires what is contrary to the Spirit, and the Spirit what is contrary to the sinful nature. They are in conflict with each other, so that *you do not do what you want*" (emphasis added).

Paul addresses believers—people who possess the Spirit and are commanded to obey—to be holy. But these same people, who love God and want to express his character, also have a sinful nature imbedded in them. This nature or tendency is so deep that becoming a new person in Christ doesn't fully eradicate it. Even when we want to do right, we sometimes don't. We want holiness, we strive for it, and we fail. The Bible tells us so.

We still have that sinful nature, but we also have the Spirit of God to lead, guide, and empower us. Quite a contradictory combination, isn't it? Perhaps our lie comes from a desire for life to be black and white, all one or the other. But if we agree "consistency is the hobgoblin of small minds," then we can begin to understand how the two can coexist in us.

GRACE AS GLUE

Perhaps we can think of grace as the glue that binds these together. Grace acknowledges the deadliness of sin. If sin weren't a reality in our lives we would never need grace. Grace provides the forgiveness that takes away the guilt of our sin. Grace is the only solution to the presence of sin in our lives.

Grace, however, also takes dealing with sin out of the arena of our having to be perfect. We rely on grace, not on our power to conquer sin. We strive to be holy *as a result* of what God freely offers us in grace. We don't earn grace; it's given. But we do yearn for holiness to best match the grace we've received.

Do you see how grace combines the dual realities of our need for holiness and the ongoing presence of sin in our lives? Both are real. The lie arrives when we deny the reality that sin continues to be present in us. That's the truth. Now, how can we live in accord with it?

Live the Truth

Let me suggest four "easy" steps that will allow us to live in the truth and to avoid the lie that we must be perfect. I put "easy" in quotes to acknowledge that I realize living these out is much more difficult than writing them down! This lie comes with a multitude of excuses and struggles, so let's address each of them.

ACKNOWLEDGE THE LIE

Abandon perfectionism. Eliminate the damaging belief that "real" Christians won't do certain things. Included are acts that absolutely violate scriptural commands. Christians shouldn't commit adultery, but they do. Adultery is an exceptionally serious sin. But does that mean that a person who does it doesn't qualify as a believer? Ask King David. Denying that you follow Jesus is an exceptionally serious sin. But does that mean a person who does it doesn't qualify as a believer? Ask the apostle Peter.

We can go down the line. Christians often do many things they shouldn't, but they are still genuine believers. This doesn't excuse the sin; we'll cover that next. But don't have the unrealistic expectation that you or others just won't sin. That doesn't match Scripture or practice.

DON'T EXCUSE YOUR SIN

Here's where we get some balance. Yes, Christians shouldn't sin. Yes, Christians do sin. But does that make it okay? When the Internet came along, Sean went online. He worked as a researcher and was amazed at the good information he was able to access. But out of curiosity, he clicked onto a pornography site and gradually got hooked on it. That pervasive draw pulled him in during slow moments at work and solitary moments at home. As a solid believer the guilt overwhelmed him, but he found it almost impossible to quit.

He contacted his pastor, and together they established some guidelines and a support system. He made some good progress, but slips still occurred. Then he went off the wagon on a binge that lasted several days. Disgust finally led Sean back to his pastor, and they tried to identify what caused the backsliding.

"Pastor, you know I want to end this, but those desires still torment me. I see the pictures from the past and want to go back to them. I thought it wouldn't hurt to take a quick look. Then, I got disgusted at how quickly I got sucked back in. The temptation seems so overwhelming that I wonder if I'll ever beat it. And

I get discouraged. If I can't stop it, I might as well let it run its course. I can't help it."

That's an excuse and a lie we'll deal with in the next chapter. May we *never* use our inclination to sin to rationalize the sin we do. Intrinsically sin damages us. Every time. And although we won't ever live sin free, we can't use that as an excuse to let sin run free in our lives.

DON'T BEAT YOURSELF UP

When we buy into the lie of perfectionism, anything less tells us something about ourselves. We're not good Christians. We're perverted. We're hopeless. We don't live up to the standard because we have a major character flaw.

Sean struggled with that. He identified himself as a sex addict. Did he match the definitions? Probably. But when he thought of himself as a sex addict, it became easier to do what sex addicts do. The shame grew, the self-condemnation increased, and he lost motivation to continue the battle against sexual temptation.

Please listen carefully here. I don't want to argue against addictions and teach that all you need to do is pray to overcome them. The behavior and identity patterns are too complex to allow that. But I am concerned with identifying a person *primarily* as an addict instead of as a new creation in Christ. Remember in the Galatians 5 passage where Paul acknowledged that the sinful nature continues with us, but that we're also indwelt, filled, and empowered by God's Holy Spirit.

We can live by the Spirit. Not easily, not perfectly, but we can follow his leading. God doesn't require perfection, but progress. At what stage in your Christian life here on earth will you see perfection? You won't. But you should see overall progress.

Think back to the biblical characters we examined earlier who did some major sins. Did those sins make them feel like dog meat? For a short time perhaps, but they moved on with God. They made spiritual progress. They continued to sin, but not as severely, not as frequently.

Now, if living the truth means we don't beat ourselves up, it also impacts how we treat others.

DON'T BEAT OTHERS UP

Regrettably, Christians often have a reputation of being judgmental and critical. On the day I wrote this section, Pat Robertson of the Christian Broadcasting Network announced he was selling his racehorses. He owned a few horses and loved to see them race. However, some Christians heard about it and criticized him strongly for it. Rather than allow that to be an issue, Pat graciously decided to end his involvement with the horses.

Don't we have better things to talk about as Christians? Don't we have more important issues to address that impact the kingdom? Did God think this issue was important enough to put commands on the pages of the Bible? To his credit, Pat didn't want his owning a few horses to become a dividing issue. To the discredit of his critics, they did.

People, let's major on the majors and not on the minors. Let's not judge others on nonbiblical grounds. Listen to the encouragement Jesus gave in Matthew 7:1–5, 12:

> Do not judge, or you too will be judged. For in the same way you judge others, you will be judged, and with the measure you use, it will be measured to you. Why do you look at the speck of sawdust in your brother's eye and pay no attention to the plank in your own eye? How can you say to your brother, "Let me take the speck out of your eye," when all the time there is a plank in your own eye? You hypocrite, first take the plank out of your own eye, and then you will see clearly to remove the speck from your brother's eye…. So in everything, do to others what you would have them do to you, for this sums up the Law and the Prophets.

Often, we'll extend grace to ourselves when we sin. We understand our reasons, our vulnerabilities, and while not justifying our sin, we don't make a big thing of it. But when others sin, we haul out the artillery. We're all over them like bees on flowers. And bees sting. Sometimes we sting when people fail on scriptural issues. Sometimes, as in Pat's situation, the issues are human opinions.

Let's give grace. Not that we ignore and excuse sin, but let's avoid double standards, judging others more harshly than we judge ourselves. Let's contribute to solving the problem of sin rather than adding to a person's guilt.

Remember the pike? The fish that gave up when confronted with what seemed to be an impossible task? For us, living without sin is that impossible task. When we realize the lie of perfectionism, we can avoid giving up hope. Focus on making progress spiritually, not on becoming perfect. We can do that! And that's the truth.

Log the Truth

1. Has failing to be perfectly obedient caused spiritual discouragement? Describe your experience.

2. How do you recover when you sin? Are you able to forgive yourself?

3. Do you carry a mental list of behaviors "real" Christians don't participate in? Write it out.

4. How does your list correspond to 1 John 1:8, which says Christians *will* sin?

5. When you think of key Bible characters who sinned signifi-cantly, which person do you think of first? How did God respond to that person?

6. How does God respond to us when we sin?

7. In your own words, describe how grace bonds God's command for us to be holy and his promise we will sin.

Lie 3

We Can't Be Perfect

The Truth about Purity

The first peek at his dad's adult magazine entranced Joe at fifteen. He had never seen such beauty. Although his conscience bothered him, he eased it by rationalizing that his dad read the magazines and still led the parking ministry at church. Besides, why would God create such beauty just to keep it hidden? It wasn't long before that "first peek" developed into a habit that stayed with him through college. It took every ounce of determination he had to put it aside when he married, but he got it under control. … He thought.

Internet access at home piqued his curiosity, so he decided to "check out some sites." The pull became irresistible. Almost any spare moment provided a chance to go online and view pornography. He knew he shouldn't, but he couldn't stop. After a few years of incredible guilt, he entered an accountability relationship with a friend who battled the same problem. Curt had already achieved several years of purity.

Joe said to him, "You know, I never thought I'd get to this point. I'm a Christian; I love God and cherish my wife. But I just can't stop this. It's too strong for me. Still, I see you succeeding. Am I the only one who can't overcome this sin? I feel so hopeless."

Carolyn loved to get the latest news about her friends, neighbors, coworkers, and people from church. She earned her reputation as the "network queen." She faithfully kept each secret—at least until she had a chance to pass it on. With each tidbit of gossip, though, she felt a twinge inside. She'd read all the verses about gossip and had no doubt they included her favorite pastime. But she yearned to know the inside scoop, and good ones couldn't be kept.

In a moment of honesty she confided to a friend in her women's Bible study group: "You know, I never thought I'd get here. I'm a Christian; I love God and want to be holy in my conversation. But I just can't stop this. It's too strong for me. I see other women stop gossiping. Am I the only one who can't overcome this sin? I feel so hopeless."

Joe and Carolyn bought into the lie that some temptations are too strong for us to resist. And if we can't resist them, why bother fighting them at all? When we believe this lie, our spiritual lives lose power and purity, we miss God's best for us, and we can't seem to do anything about it.

Identify the Lie

You might notice a connection between this and the last chapter. Both deal with our failure to live the Christian life. Lie 2 focused on our misconception that God requires moral perfection, that we should never sin. We learned those standards are unrealistic. This chapter explores how some temptations seem to exceed our ability to overcome them.

In both cases we don't live up to God's standards—but with a shift in the focus. With perfectionism (described in Lie 2), the external standards are too high. Here, we face realistic standards, but we lack the internal power to reach them. To win this fight we must engage fully. This involves our spiritual power, our spiritual will, and our spiritual heart for purity.

Feelings and thoughts of powerlessness give strength to the lie that we can't successfully fight temptation. (By powerlessness, I mean apathy, a victim mentality—not the powerlessness of 12-step programs that have participants admit that they are powerless over their addictions.)

When we read the following passages we can easily develop a sense of hopelessness. Not because the standards are too high—we see others meeting them—but they're too high for us, because we don't have the power we need.

Near the end of his life, the apostle John wrote to some dear brothers and sisters to encourage them to get the most from their Christian faith. Only eight verses into his first letter, he says, "If we claim to be *without sin*, we deceive ourselves and the truth is not in us" (1 John 1:8, emphasis added). To best live as a Christian, he told us, we must admit that we fail to perfectly live the Christian life.

In case they didn't get the message, he repeated the concept in verse 10: "If we claim we have not sinned, we make him out to be a liar and his word has no place in our lives."

John seems to indicate that the key to successful spirituality is failure. No matter how "good" we get, we'll still sin. I find that both encouraging and discouraging. How about you? If not, chew on this passage from Romans 7:15–24 from the *New Living Translation*. Paul describes the battle Christians have with temptation and sin. Some experts believe he describes life before Christ, while others think Paul describes our current battle.

> I don't understand myself at all, for I really want to do what is right, but I don't do it. *Instead, I do the very thing I hate.* I know perfectly well that what I am doing is wrong, and my bad conscience shows that I agree that the law is good. But *I can't help myself, because it is sin inside me* that makes me do these evil things.
>
> I know I am rotten through and through so far as my old sinful nature is concerned. *No matter which way I turn, I can't make myself do right.* I want to, but I can't. When I want to do good, I don't. And when I try not to do wrong, I do it

anyway. But if I am doing what I don't want to do, I am not really the one doing it; the sin within me is doing it.

It seems to be a fact of life that *when I want to do what is right, I inevitably do what is wrong*. I love God's law with all my heart. But there is another law at work within me that is at war with my mind. This law wins the fight and makes me a slave to the sin that is still within me. Oh, what a miserable person I am! Who will free me from this life that is dominated by sin? (emphasis added).

Since the Christian life includes sin, and since faith, rather than good behavior, saves us, and since God's grace is greater than our sin, many Christians give up the battle. I can identify with that dilemma. I've fought some battles over and over. I want to do what's right but don't.

Powerlessness says that some temptations are just too strong, that we can't live without sinning. And that's a lie.

Learn the Truth

God provides all the resources we need for spiritual victory. We can conquer any temptation. Do we? Sometimes yes, sometimes no. Can we? Absolutely. Then why don't we?

Some time ago I heard the parable of Howard, a midwestern farmer who grabbed a length of rope and rode his horse down to the local Chevrolet dealer where he bought the newest, fastest, most loaded Corvette convertible he could find. He tied off the rope to the car and headed home. He parked his new sports car in his huge barn, which was equipped with an epoxy painted floor and ceiling fans. He often sat in the luxurious seats, holding his portable radio and listening to his favorite country music.

Frequently, he'd invite all his friends over for a picnic in the barn. They'd sit and admire the clean lines of the car for hours. "Howard, that car deserves a speeding ticket just sitting there." And every so often he'd hitch up the horse and pull the

'Vette for a mile or so, marveling at how smoothly it moved down the road behind the horse. He scrupulously checked the fluid levels and made sure all the belts and hoses stayed in good shape. Sometimes Howard would arrive late for worship services at the small country church: polishing the car and hitching up the horse took some time! Every so often, when the preacher got long-winded, Howard let his mind wonder what V8 power would feel like.

We have more in common with Howard than we'd like to think.

THE PROMISE

God assures us that he provides the power we need to reach his standards. Like Howard, we already have what we need. Whereas Howard adjusted belts and hoses, we need to begin with an attitude adjustment, one that deals with how we view temptation, sin, and spiritual victory. Think carefully about the promise in 1 Corinthians 10:13: "*No temptation has seized you except what is common to man. And God is faithful; he will not let you be tempted beyond what you can bear. But when you are tempted, he will also provide a way out so that you can stand up under it*" (emphasis added).

First, Paul makes it clear that no temptation we face is any worse than any temptation another person may face.

An uncle abused Vic sexually when Vic was in his early teens, and the incident changed the course of the boy's life. Vic's premature exposure to sex led him into a variety of sexual sins, but he loved God and felt tremendous guilt over the ways in which he fulfilled his desires. Then in a men's group, another man talked about his sexual struggle and how he'd been able to grow beyond the temptations.

They met later, and Vic expressed his relief. "Jack, I'm amazed. I thought I was the only Christian man to face these things. You don't know how much it helps me to know that others have dealt with this and won."

Second, God promises to limit the level of temptation to what we can handle. He considers our level of spiritual maturity, experience, and faith. Though I certainly feel overwhelmed by some temptations, God says he'll make sure he doesn't give us anything we can't deal with.

Third, if a temptation threatens to exceed our ability to deal with it, God will provide an escape route. I love the story of Joseph back in Genesis 39. Joseph was the steward of an official's house, and the man's wife kept hitting on him. He tried to avoid her, but when everyone else was out of the house, she grabbed him by his robe, saying, "Come to bed with me!" Not very subtle.

He'd tried to reason with her before, and I suspect the pressure to give in was getting pretty high. So what did he do? He used the escape route; he ran and left his cloak in her hands.

Remember the great encouragement we received earlier from the apostle John—that we will sin? John lived in the real world. Though his circumstances were different, he faced difficulties just like we do. He undoubtedly struggled with the same realities Paul described in Romans 7. But he also knew the promise God has given us, and he wrote the entire letter of 1 John to burn that purpose into our minds: "My dear children, I write this to you *so that you will not sin*" (2:1, emphasis added).

Even though we must deal daily with temptations, and even though many of them seem to possess the power of a nuclear explosion, John wants us to know we can win. So, when we face temptations like Joe and Carolyn did, the ones that tend to beat us up time after time, let's reprogram our minds with this promise: We can stand against any temptation.

But how?

THE POWER

Two contradictory forces work on our lives. Before we come to Christ, the sinful nature predominates. We may hunger for God, feel the conviction of his Spirit, and strive to do good, but the grip of our predisposition to sin holds firmly to us. Galatians 5:16–17 expresses that: "So I say, live by the Spirit, and you will not gratify the desires of the sinful nature. For the sinful nature desires what is contrary to the Spirit, and the Spirit what is contrary to the sinful nature. They are in conflict with each other, so that you do not do what you want."

When we come to Christ, however, the balance of power changes, according to verse 24: *"Those who belong to Christ Jesus have crucified the sinful nature* with its passions and desires" (emphasis added).

Conversion breaks the overwhelming grip of sin. Not only does our old sinful nature get broken, we gain elements of a new nature. Second Peter 1:4 says, "He has given us his very great and precious promises, so that through them *you may participate in the divine nature* and escape the corruption in the world caused by evil desires" (emphasis added).

Without getting into all that "participating in the divine nature" entails, understand that Peter is not saying we become divine. But God gives us some of his nature, which allows us to break the power of temptation. That means that we become a new creation, a new person. Our very nature changes, according to 2 Corinthians 5:17: "Therefore, if anyone is in Christ, he is a new creation; the old has gone, the new has come!"

The old nature, dominated by an inability to win against temptation, has been put to death. We've taken on part of God's nature to the point of becoming a new creation. We're not what we were before. We're not helpless victims at the absent mercy of sin. Because we are a new creation empowered by God, the power of our sin nature has died.

That's great news. But why don't we live like that? We need that attitude adjustment, we need to understand the power resident within us, and we need to realize that practical victory over sin is a lifelong journey.

THE PROCESS

John gave us tremendous insights into the reality of sin and spiritual success. Yes, we will sin, but we don't have to! God has provided for us a strategy with which we avoid problems like those Joe and Carolyn faced, as well as many others.

We live in an age of instant satisfaction. We want what we want, how we want it, and when. Microwaves, instant coffee, fast food, and broadband Internet connections all feed our "need for speed." So when we begin our spiritual journey, we expect to instantly slay spiritual dragons. We forget that knights need training.

In the real world, we'll fight temptation our entire lives. We'll never arrive at perfection, as we learned in the last chapter, but we can continually improve as dragon fighters. We gain that victory by the process called sanctification. A passage in Hebrews 10 helps explain the two. Verse 10 says, "*We have been made holy* through the sacrifice of the body of Jesus Christ once for all" (emphasis added).

Notice that we have been made holy—past tense. Action finished. And if we stopped there, we could easily fall prey to perfectionism. God has made us holy; task completed. We never have to sin again. Since that's not how most of us live, let's go on. Verse 14 has the rest of the story: "... because by one sacrifice he has made perfect forever *those who are being made holy*" (emphasis added).

Hold on a moment. Verse 10 said we're already holy, but verse 14 says we're still in the process of holiness. God, get it straight. Are we holy or not? Yes and no. When we accept Christ, we're clothed with Christ's holiness, and that's what God sees. But in practice, have we completed the change into holy lives? Not yet. The battle rages on.

God has changed our nature. He assures our eventual victory over sin, but we still have battles to fight. We still need to improve as dragon slayers. We'll eventually kill all the dragons, but we can expect to be wounded by claws, teeth, and fiery breath.

Second Corinthians 3:18 exquisitely expresses that tension: "And we all ... are being changed into his likeness from one degree of glory to another" (RSV, emphasis added).

God continues to transform us into his likeness, step by step. We begin with some glory, grow, and become more spiritually glorious. Then we slip, lose a bit of glory, but we get back on track and pick up some more. And that goes on until we reach heaven.

We shouldn't expect to be perfect. Nor should we expect every temptation to knock us flat. We should expect to win some battles. We should expect to lose some. We should expect to win more and lose fewer as God continues to transform us into the likeness of Christ.

God provides the process by which we learn to stand against temptation. We possess all the weapons we need. Now, how do we use those weapons?

Live the Truth

We begin with a heart check. What do we want most of all? To win, we need to yearn to become a dragon slayer, regardless of the potential for injury.

DESIRE PURITY

Think back to Joe's friendship with Curt and the struggle they shared with pornography. As Curt listened to Joe share his experiences in beating this dragon, he grew skeptical. Oh, Joe knew it was wrong, that he should stop. But every reason he came up with to stop was balanced by how much he enjoyed it and how difficult he found it to let it go.

Having been there, Curt cut to the chase. "Joe, you'll never beat this until you want it more than continuing with the porn. You need a hunger for purity. Purity isn't perfection, but making progress. Purity comes from wanting to be a man of God more than anything else and vigorously striving to reach that goal. And until you make that choice, this dragon will keep eating you alive."

Decision time. Do we battle a particular temptation, one that consistently eats us for lunch? Then we need to decide for purity. Right now. We choose the direction toward purity and away from further sin. Why? Because we're children of God. God is holy, and regular kids want to be like their dad.

"But just as he who called you is holy, so be holy in all you do; for it is written: *'Be holy, because I am holy'* " (1 Peter 1:15-16, emphasis added).

Don't get seduced into thinking God requires perfection. Also, avoid the seduction of powerlessness. We begin the process of purity when we decide to become as much like God as we can. Part of us may love pornography or gossip or envy or greed, and that desire may stick with us the rest of our lives. But we need to love God more. That's what gets us started.

ACKNOWLEDGE FAILURES

We defeat both perfectionism and powerlessness by living in the truth. When we fail, we admit it. Only lately have I discovered the freedom that comes with saying, "I was wrong. I sinned against you. Will you forgive me?" That breaks the curse of pretending to be perfect and reminds me that I need more of God's power.

Let's go back to more of John's real-life advice. He wrote the book because we sin, but so we wouldn't. So when we sin, what do we do? "If we confess our sins, he is faithful and just and *will forgive us* our sins and *purify us* from all unrighteousness" (1 John 1:9, emphasis added).

Here comes purity again! Yes, we sin, but when we acknowledge it to God and relevant others, he not only forgives us, but puts us back on the purity track. Not perfectionism, but purity. Not powerlessness, but power to move beyond those sins.

Along with confession comes our need to receive forgiveness from God and from ourselves. I've found that Satan uses his most effective weapon when he merely reminds me of wrong things I've done. Guilt, shame, and embarrassment flood through me. I feel unworthy even to be a Christian, let alone attempt to serve my Savior. Maybe you've felt that shame from losing the same battles over and over. You want to give up in discouragement and hopelessness. Each new failure multiplies the total amount of guilt. And even though we've confessed it to God, we've prayed and asked others to pray for us, we still feel the burden of our past sins. They're real to us, and they're fresh.

Every time we think that guilt is real, we call God a liar. Didn't John say that God forgives us? Why do we then feel unforgiven? Apparently, we don't believe God. Instead, we believe the whispers of Satan and our unrelenting feelings. Yet God gives us the solid promise that when we confess our sins, we are forgiven. Fact. Reality.

I've found I can turn Satan's tool on him. Each time he reminds me of a past sin, I pray, "God, thanks for this reminder that you have forgiven me. You promised I'm not that person anymore."

If we want to journey on the purity track, we need to grasp the freshness of forgiveness. Lamentations 3:22–23 reminds us: "Because of the LORD's great love we are not consumed, for *his compassions never fail.* They are new every morning; great is your faithfulness" (emphasis added).

God's compassion starts fresh each day. We can use the sunrise as a memory tool, thanking God each morning for his forgiveness, his compassion, and his love that allow a new beginning every day. Believe that, remember that, and live that.

REMEMBER OUR RESOURCES

Yes, we do battle some temptations over and over. Yes, we lose some battles. But never give in to the lie that we cannot resist temptation. We've already seen the resources God provides for us. We can't fully use all of them instantly; we need to learn how to use each piece of the knight's armor to fight the dragons. We need to learn the battle skills. Let's close this chapter with another longer passage, Romans 8:31–39, as an encouragement to view ourselves as already conquerors over temptation. Yes, the battle runs our entire lives. But in Christ, we're on the winning side.

> What, then, shall we say in response to this? *If God is for us, who can be against us?* He who did not spare his own Son, but gave him up for us all—how will he not also, along with him, graciously give us all things? Who will bring any charge against those whom God has chosen? It is God who justifies. Who is he that condemns? Christ Jesus, who died—more than that, who was raised to life—is at the right hand of God and is also interceding for us. Who shall separate

us from the love of Christ? Shall trouble or hardship or persecution or famine or nakedness or danger or sword? As it is written: "For your sake we face death all day long; we are considered as sheep to be slaughtered." No, in all these things *we are more than conquerors* through him who loved us. For I am convinced that neither death nor life, neither angels nor demons, neither the present nor the future, nor any powers, neither height nor depth, nor anything else in all creation, will be able to separate us from the love of God that is in Christ Jesus our Lord (emphasis added).

That's a pretty exhaustive list of forces that cannot overwhelm us without our permission. God gives us all the power we need to conquer any temptation. And that's the truth.

Log the Truth

1. What temptations seem too strong for you to resist?

2. What excuses have you created to rationalize your choices?

3. What are some "escape routes" God has provided to help you deal with strong temptations?

4. Do you find that understanding holiness as a process encourages you? Explain why or why not.

5. When you think of the temptation you struggle with the most, do you deeply desire God's best in that area of your life? If not, how can you begin to want that more than the sin?

Lie 4

Little Sins Aren't Really That Bad

The Truth about Sin's Damage

Stephen ran his own business, and much of his income came in the form of cash. Every year well before tax time, he carefully put together his income and deductions. He compared both to what he'd done the year before and reported just enough to appear consistent. By doing so, he could safely underreport his income and save thousands in taxes.

He'd heard the pastor's sermon that we should pay our full taxes, but he shrugged off his deceit: "Well, most people do the same, and the government just wastes most of it anyway."

Colleen loved to shop. She and her husband George had agreed on a budget that included some money for personal use for each of them even though they had little to spare once the bills were paid. Despite the tightness of their finances, however, Colleen just couldn't say no to some "deals." Once she couldn't resist the beauty of a diamond necklace. Another time she couldn't pass up Nordstrom's price on a coat. She regularly blew the budget. Big time.

George had to figure out how to juggle bills to pay these unexpected expenses, and that brought financial stress to the family. Colleen's response? "Well, I know I shouldn't do it, but it really isn't that big of a deal. Besides, I just love to shop. Walking through the stores helps me relax. I need this, and I deserve it."

Stephen and Colleen bought into the lie that little sins really don't hurt us. They're not that bad.

Identify the Lie

Perhaps you've done the same, minimizing wrong acts to excuse them. We often see people continue in a sin for years with no apparent consequences. Or we see so much sin around us that it becomes just a regular part of the landscape of life. While we know that sins are wrong, we don't see the small ones as a terminal disease.

Once again, we can find Scripture to support our misconception.

SALVATION BY FAITH

Mac eagerly embraced the good news of Jesus and quickly memorized Ephesians 2:8–9 as the focus of his new faith. He loved the freedom found in the promise, "For it is by grace you have been saved, through faith—and this not from yourselves, it is the gift of God—not by works, so that no one can boast."

He understood that we cannot be saved by being good, but only by the grace of God. But he took that separation of works from salvation into the everyday Christian life. He reasoned, "If being good can't save me, then it can't influence my living as a Christian." He lived consistent with that belief.

He cheated on his wife before becoming a Christian, and he did the same after. He didn't go to church before, and he didn't after. He took advantage of people before, and he did the same after. Eventually he left his wife and children for someone else, always proclaiming that he'd been saved by grace and walked with Christ. He never thought that sins could hurt his faith.

Because he looked at just part of Scripture, Mac divorced actions from faith. He missed that next verse, which says, "For we are God's workmanship, created in Christ Jesus *to do good works*, which God prepared in advance for us to do" (v. 10, emphasis added).

He missed Jesus' statement: "If you love me, *you will obey* what I command" (John 14:15, emphasis added). Mac minimized sin because of an incomplete understanding of what it means to be saved by grace.

FREEDOM IN CHRIST

Others minimize sin because they misunderstand our freedom in Christ. We can easily do that, as did the church in Galatia. They took their freedom from having to follow the law a few steps too far, and Paul had to rein them in just a bit in 5:13: "You, my brothers, were called to be free. But *do not use your freedom to indulge the sinful nature*" (emphasis added).

Why did Paul have to say that? Apparently, they did use their freedom from law as an excuse for sin. They seemed to think that if God gave them freedom, then God allowed them to do whatever they desired. Freedom in Christ means we have the ability to achieve God's design for us. Freedom doesn't mean we're free to sin, rather we become free to say no to sin. But if we miss this distinction, we become vulnerable to the lie.

ABUNDANT FORGIVENESS

I sometimes think forgiveness is too easy. Here's why. From 1 John 1:9: "If we *confess our sins*, he is faithful and just and *will forgive us our sins* and purify us from all unrighteousness" (emphasis added). We gain forgiveness from any sin merely by acknowledging to God that we sinned. "Yeah, God, you're right. That was a sin. We're cool now, right?"

How often can we work the process? Here's what the Bible says: "Then Peter came to Jesus and asked, 'Lord, how many times shall I forgive my brother when he sins against me? Up to seven times?' Jesus answered, 'I tell you, not seven times, but seventy-seven times'" (Matthew 18:21–22).

I learned that as seventy times seven or 490 times. But either way—49 or 490—I would soon run out of fingers and toes. Jesus didn't mean to give a specific limit, but to tell us that we can't exhaust the abundance of God's forgiveness.

Many of us assume then, that sin can't be too bad if God forgives us so easily. We minimize our sin; we just don't think it's that bad. Yes, we agree it's wrong, but not *that* wrong.

We need to discover God's view on the seriousness of sin.

Learn the Truth

If you cheated a little by looking at the table of contents, you know that both this chapter and the next deal with inaccurate perceptions of sin. This chapter examines how we minimize sin; the next explores how we maximize sin. Two very different slants, but they share some common truth, so some of what we now look at will also provide a foundation for the next chapter.

DEFINING SIN

The starting point for a more complete understanding of sin comes with seeing its essence. Most of us have heard that sin comes from an archery term that means "to miss the mark." We sin when we miss God's target. Typically we think the target includes the specifics from the Ten Commandments or the teachings of the New Testament: don't commit sexual sin; don't steal; practice hospitality, and more. You probably know most of the rest of the list!

LESS THAN OUR BEST

God, however, gives us a much broader target. Someone asked Jesus about what one target we should aim for. Jesus replied, "Love the Lord your God with all your heart and with all your soul and with all your mind.' This is the first and greatest commandment. And the second is like it: 'Love your neighbor as yourself.' All the Law and the Prophets hang on these two commandments" (Matthew 22:37-40).

Follow the trail of logic here. We sin if we don't hit the target. The target is to love God with all our being and to love others as ourselves. All other commands flow from that. We sin when we do anything less. Anytime we love God with less than our best, we sin. Anytime we don't best express love to others, we sin. Doesn't that expand our perception of sin?

Paul gives another slant on that principle in Romans 14:23: "Everything that does not come from faith is sin." If I don't do something as a positive expression of my faith, then I sin. I may do the "right thing," but if I haven't thought it through and made sure my motive is to express faith, then I miss the target. Even if I do the right thing!

REBELLION TOWARD GOD

We still haven't hit all that contributes to the essence of sin. Most of us know the story of the Prodigal Son. The young man asked his father to give him his inheritance early; he received it, became a party animal, and lost it all. He finally came to his senses and returned to his father. He recognized the seriousness of his sin and wanted only to be a worker on his father's farm. "Father, I have sinned against heaven and against you. I am no longer worthy to be called your son" (Luke 15:21).

What was his sin? Rebelling against the father. What brought restoration? A change of attitude.

The essence of sin is not treating God as our Father, as Lord, as preeminent. Rather than sin primarily being a specific act, sin involves our attitude toward God. We sin when we think we know better than God. We sin when we'd rather follow our desires than his. That's why sin is so serious.

Damage from Sin

Sin always brings damage. That damage may come immediately or later. That damage may be subtle or obvious. But it will affect our lives in a number of destructive manners.

DESTRUCTION TO SELF

At the very core, sin brings damage to us when we do it. I used to think of God as a cosmic spoilsport—he told me not to do everything that seemed fun! Rules served only to see if I would obey. They were arbitrary, meaningless, an exertion of power. I could usually see no purpose behind them. Besides, what God called sin certainly looked attractive! The writer of Hebrews talks about how a person can choose "to enjoy the pleasures of sin" (Hebrews 11:25). He goes on to say that those pleasures only last for a short time.

In truth, the pleasures of sin only mask the underlying destruction. Think carefully about the warning in 1 Peter 5:8: "Be self-controlled and alert. Your enemy the devil prowls around like a roaring lion looking for someone to devour." When Satan seeks to entice us, he offers pleasure, but he gives damage.

I like what the science fiction writer Piers Anthony said: "Satan is an insidious corrupter who never rests, and he is most dangerous in seeming defeat. It is his specialty to proffer a large reward (our pleasure) for a very small compromise ... it then becomes easier to accept the next, and the next, until at last Satan has won."

We always need to remember that Satan doesn't desire our best, merely our destruction. And any sin can move us further down that road.

DIMINISHED RELATIONSHIPS WITH PEOPLE

Charlie Brown built a sand castle at the beach, and Lucy promptly came over, ruined it, and then apologized. "I'm sorry, Charlie Brown, I won't do it again." So, trusting Charlie Brown built another, and Lucy returned with the same result. Once again she apologized. But did Lucy's bad behavior—even with an apology—help or hurt their relationship?

Each time we wrong a person, we injure our relationship with him or her. Sometimes we can just slough it off. Sometimes one injury does long-term damage. Sometimes a number of small events accumulate and create a large impact. But because sin misses the mark of giving our best love, it inherently brings less than the best to our relationships.

I think that's why Jesus encouraged us to not allow our sins to continue to bring damage to one another. "If your brother sins against you, go and show him his fault, just between the two of you. If he listens to you, you have won your brother over" (Matthew 18:15). In other words, don't allow the initial "missing the mark of love" to keep damaging relationships.

DISTANCE FROM GOD

Some time ago I allowed a particular sin too much room in my life. I knew it was wrong and wanted to end it, but not enough. Over the months that it continued, I saw my intimacy with God decrease. Worship especially became difficult. How could I praise God as ultimate when I clearly disobeyed him?

I could only change that direction when I changed my behavior. When I did change, that former closeness began to return. Notice that word *began*. The damage from months of sin took time to move beyond. Yes, I received forgiveness as soon as I confessed and repented, but it took some time to recover from the consequences.

What bothered me the most through all of that? I knew sin creates distance. I want to love God more than anything else, I yearn to get closer, but I knowingly allowed that sin to interfere. I knew well the warning found in Isaiah 59:2: "But your iniquities have separated you from your God; your sins have hidden his face from you, so that he will not hear."

SPIRITUAL DEPRESSION

Along with distance, sin brings the spiritual blahs. Not only are we distant, we feel distant, we feel hopeless. In the previous example, I felt like spiritual quicksand trapped my entire life. Again, that's a biblical result of sin. "Our offenses and sins weigh us down, and we are wasting away because of them. How then can we live?" (Ezekiel 33:10).

The more sin we allow into our lives, the lower our emotional health. Sin is the 800-pound gorilla we carry that keeps us from soaring spiritually.

DEATH OF JESUS

Overall, the greatest damage from sin deals with the necessity of Christ's death. Anytime we begin to think that sins really aren't that bad, we need to consider the cost: God's Son had to give his life for us. Each sin of mine was another blow to the spikes that pierced his hands and feet. His good friend Peter knew that and expressed it well: "*He himself bore our sins* in his body on the tree, so that we might die to sins and live for righteousness; *by his wounds you have been healed*" (1 Peter 2:24, emphasis added).

The cost of our surly attitude to a waitress: the death of God's Son. The cost of our gossip: the death of God's Son. The cost of our lust: the death of God's Son. The cost of our greed: the death of God's Son. The cost of our self-centeredness: the death of God's Son.

OUR SPIRITUAL DEATH

If we don't take advantage of Jesus' dying for us, we receive an even greater personal cost: "For the wages of sin is death" (Romans 6:23). Because sin is essentially rebellion against who God is, it brings an everlasting separation from him. Sin brings eternity spent in hell. How we deal with our sinfulness determines our future. Apart from Christ paying the penalty we've fully earned, we have no means of dealing with sin. We're destined to die spiritually. For us individually, we can find no greater cost.

If sin didn't bring pleasure, we wouldn't do it so often! Let's not minimize the pleasure. But let's also not minimize the damage that always comes with sin. When we put them both on a balance scale, that damage greatly outweighs the pleasure. Too often in my past, I've tried to tell myself that my sins really weren't that bad. Maybe you've done the same. In truth, they are that bad—and even worse.

Live the Truth

How will our lives change when we accept the truth of these principles? Let's examine three steps.

ACCEPT THE TRUTH

Too often we believe things in our head, but those beliefs don't work their way into our deep-seated attitudes. It is possible, however, to imbed the truth of sin's consequences into our values. We can think about them when we face temptation. We can counter the seductions of pleasure.

After fifteen years of struggling in marriage, Mark felt ready to give up. Margie seemed consumed with her activities and had withdrawn emotionally. They'd gone through three bouts of marital counseling, and each felt like a fifteen-round championship match fought to a draw. Mark began to think about the advantages of divorce, which initially seemed pretty obvious: The kids wouldn't be poisoned by a terrible example of marriage;

Margie could freely pursue her interests; and he could seek a more satisfying companion.

But Mark knew that God hates divorce (Malachi 2:16), and he thought he ought to explore what that really meant before he made any final decisions. He studied what the Bible said about marriage, separation, forgiveness, restoration, and divorce. He talked to his pastor. He talked to friends who'd gone through divorce. He talked to friends with difficult marriages who emerged from their struggles not just together but closer. He talked to friends who struggled in their marriages but stayed in them anyway, still frustrated. He read the studies about the short- and long-term impacts of divorce on both the adults and the children.

Mark began to understand God's perspective on the devastation that divorce brings. He saw how marriage joins two people into one and how divorce rips them apart, back into two. He learned that a good marriage provides a safe harbor where we can admit our weaknesses, still be loved, and grow beyond them. Divorce thrusts us into a world of isolation and insecurity. Mark discovered how a good marriage provides a secure foundation for children to develop, to pattern themselves after the male and female roles expressed by their parents.

He talked to Margie about the options they faced, the advantages and disadvantages of each, and they began working together more closely. Until then, they hadn't explored the consequences of continuing with an unsatisfactory marriage or divorce. They found a third alternative that didn't have the costs of the others.

They accepted the truth and sought God's best.

BUILD A HOLY HATRED

For much of my life, I've accepted evil as part of the landscape. Something to avoid, certainly. Something wrong, no doubt. Something that missed God's best, absolutely. But I relied on God's grace and tolerated evil much more than I should have.

Earlier in the chapter I talked about a sin I allowed and its resulting devastation. I've now solidly planted that sin in the past, but victory only came when I built a holy disgust toward the sin and the damage it brought to people I loved, to me, and to God's kingdom. Until then, the pleasures seemed to outweigh the cost. I don't want to be that person anymore. I can truly say I hate that activity and never want it in my life again. Am I still tempted by its pleasures? Yes. But now I know the cost, and it's too high.

I discovered a passage that expresses the dual approach to overcoming sin, "*Hate what is evil*; cling to what is good" (Romans 12:9, emphasis added). My problem before? I wanted to cling to good. I truly did. I fought the temptation regularly. But I didn't hate the evil. I didn't recognize the innate damage that sin brings. I wish I'd written this chapter six years ago and avoided all this pain!

FLEE FROM SIN

I couldn't truly do this until I built a holy hatred for sin. The evil of sin had to exceed the pleasures for me to successfully build the motivation I needed. Once we have that intense disgust for sin and its results in our lives, we can then move away. In 1 Timothy 6:5-10 Paul talks about how the love of money can seduce us. Then he takes the principle a step further in verse 11: "But you, man of God, *flee from all this* [all kinds of evil], and pursue righteousness, godliness, faith, love, endurance and gentleness" (emphasis added).

Notice the active tense: flee from all evil; pursue righteousness. What do you need to flee from? What form of righteousness do you need to pursue? Do it. Like Todd Beamer.

I greatly admired Todd's role in keeping the September 11 terrorists from crashing United Flight 93 into another building. But that didn't come close to what may been his most difficult and heroic act. In *Let's Roll*, his widow, Lisa, told of Todd's workaholism, how his intense Type A personality drove him to success. Manifested first during their dating, that trait continued into their marriage. Adored by his children and cherished by his wife, he still found it difficult to say no to work demands.

Eventually he realized his behavior didn't allow him to love and serve God with all he had. He couldn't lovingly meet the needs of his wife and children as he should. He saw the damage it brought, called it sin, and changed it. That transformed his marriage and how he interacted with his children. Todd realized that sin brings damage. Always. And that's the truth.

Log the Truth

1. Which sins in your life have you minimized?

2. What attitudes toward sin have allowed you to minimize its wrongness?

3. Have you taken unfair advantage of forgiveness? How?

4. This chapter presents a broad definition of sin that relates to the Greatest Commandment. Do you agree with it? Why or why not?

5. Which of the six areas of sin's damage have you experienced? What were the circumstances?

6. Do you truly hate evil? How can you increase your godly hatred of it?

Lie 5

One Sin Does Destroy Us

The Truth about Forgiveness and Restoration

In the movie *Les Miserables,* stealing food cost Jean Valjean nineteen years of freedom. Even after his release from prison, his status as a convict chased him relentlessly. Although he became a prosperous and charitable businessman, the consequences of his past continued. One act changed the course of his life.

After growing up in church and getting burned once or twice as a young adult, Daryl went his own way. He dropped one failed marriage and way too many beer bottles on that path before meeting his second wife. Further tragedy struck when his mother died.

Devastated, Daryl started to think about things he'd ignored for decades. Although his mom put God at the core of her life, he didn't know where God fit into his. He just knew she died in peace, and he wasn't even close to that. The ferment forced him to reevaluate how he lived. He went back to church, and his faith blossomed.

The foundation of those early years helped Daryl to grow quickly. His common sense and practical bent, now sensitized by the Spirit, made him a valuable advisor to his pastor. After ten years, Pastor Bob wanted to make it official and asked if Daryl would pray about serving as an elder in the church.

Daryl struggled with a theological issue, and the two discussed it at length. "Bob, I can't get over the verse that says an elder must be the husband of one wife. I know God forgave me; I have no doubt about that. But I've had two wives. I just don't think I'm qualified."

The situations of both Valjean and Daryl represent a lie that many of us succumb to: The effects of sin are too damaging to overcome. Our lives bear a taint that remains despite forgiveness.

Identify the Lie

This chapter flips the coin from the last chapter. There, we saw how easily we can *minimize* sin and pretend it doesn't damage us too much. Sin becomes a sleeping kitten that we tiptoe past. Here, we easily *maximize* sin and think we can never overcome its consequences. Sin becomes a roaring lion that's got us cornered.

As we learned, sin brings damage. Always. That damage can be quite severe, bringing devastation *to us,* lessening the quality of our lives.

> •Sin diminishes relationships: it increases the friction between people.

> •Sin causes us to experience a feeling of separation from God: it decreases our intimacy when we rebel toward him.

> •Sin leads to spiritual depression: our spirits feel stuck as if in quicksand.

> •Sin required the death of Jesus: God had no other options to deal with our sin.

> •Sin results in our own spiritual death: we are eternally separated from God unless we accept Christ's death for us.

We often see one act negatively impact the rest of a life. David, the second king of Israel, had an adulterous affair with a neighbor's wife. When she became pregnant, he used the power of his position to kill her husband to keep the deed secret. God seems to have given David a year to acknowledge this wrong, but David blissfully enjoyed his new wife and son—until God sent a prophet named Nathan to deliver a message: David's act would change his life.

> Now, therefore, *the sword will never depart* from your house, because you despised me and took the wife of Uriah the Hittite to be your own ... Out of your own household I am going to bring calamity upon you. Before your very eyes I will take your wives and give them to one who is close to you, and he will lie with your wives in broad daylight. You did it *in secret*, but I will do this thing in *broad daylight* before all Israel (2 Samuel 12:10–12, emphasis added).

David battled the rest of his life; his own son even led a rebellion against him. Why? David's sin opened a Pandora's box of violence that he couldn't close.

Some acts irrevocably change our lives. Cheryl and Chris began dating as sophomores in high school, and their romance continued as they attended a local state college. Enraptured with each other, neither even considered other attachments. After graduation they married and moved to a nearby state for Chris's new job. Cheryl enjoyed both of the kids they soon had, but slowly she began to wonder if she'd missed anything. She'd never even dated anyone else.

When the checker at the local market gently flirted with her, she surprised herself by not just noticing it, but quietly enjoying it. She found herself going to the market to just "pick up some fresh vegetables" more frequently, and she always got in Gene's line. The flirting exploded into a full-blown affair that thrilled her beyond imagination. She felt more alive, more whole, and more of a woman than ever before.

She soon abandoned Chris and the kids and moved in with Gene. But within a year she learned that Gene flirted with everyone, and he didn't stop there. Too embarrassed to tell anyone, Cheryl tried to make it work for several years. By the time she fully recognized her mistake, Chris had remarried. Cheryl looked back with nothing but regret at her decisions: she lost her husband, her children, and her childhood dreams. But she couldn't go back.

We've all seen similar situations—people make bad decisions and their lives are never the same. I've known people who drank too much before driving, and killed someone. Friends back in the 60s used mind-altering drugs that permanently damaged their minds.

Most of us know sin brings damage, but we've chosen sin anyway and experienced the devastation. We saw God opening a door for us, we went the other way, and we wonder if that choice condemns us to God's second best for the rest of our lives.

In no way do I wish to diminish the severity, wrongness, and damage of sin. I've experienced too much of that in my life, and I know I will again. Nor do I wish any of us to believe that once we sin we become damaged goods that God can't use. That we're forced to settle for God's second best. Or third, or fourth, or … That's a lie.

Learn the Truth

Rather than falling into the lie of minimizing sin, we can balance the very real damage of sin with the twin truths of forgiveness and restoration. God is a God of second chances. And third chances. And fourth chances. And so on.

Let's return to the story of David. Remember how he used violence to try to hide his sin? Yet once God confronted him through Nathan, David saw his sin, confessed it, and experienced God's grace.

> Then David said to Nathan, "*I have sinned* against the LORD." Nathan replied, "The LORD has taken away your sin. *You are not going to die.* But because by doing this you have made the enemies of the LORD show utter contempt, the

son born to you will die" (2 Samuel 12:13–14, emphasis added).

Consequences continued from the sin. But God forgave the guilt. Now, the big question: Did that *very* serious sin invalidate David from serving God? Absolutely not.

After that sin, David continued to lead the nation of Israel both politically and spiritually. He continued to write psalms, which became incorporated into Scripture. He reached out to persecuted groups in his kingdom. He planned and gathered the materials for the glorious temple of God to be built by his son Solomon. A major sin didn't eliminate David's ability to serve God.

Not long ago, my wife and I attended a Weekend to Remember conference led by Family Life Ministries. One speaker told how he'd neglected his wife to the point that she said she'd lost all feelings for him. Their marriage teetered on the brink of dissolution, but he acknowledged his failings. They changed how they treated one another, and now both lead marriage enrichment conferences. A major sin didn't eliminate them from serving God.

I wonder if Promise Keepers would have ever begun or reached so many people if God hadn't convicted Bill McCartney of how he'd failed in his life. Winning a college football championship didn't bring satisfaction, but influencing men for God did. A major sin didn't eliminate him from serving God.

Haven't we all seen people who sinned greatly, yet who God was able to use greatly? What's the secret? Let's examine two important biblical principles.

ABUNDANT FORGIVENESS

God wants all people to be as close to him as possible. Since our sin creates an impassable distance between him and us, he's put in place an offer of abundant forgiveness to bridge that gap. Jesus describes it: "I tell you the truth, *all the sins and blasphemies of men will be forgiven* them" (Mark 3:28, emphasis added). Now that's abundant!

The simple means to receive forgiveness is confession: We agree with God that what we did was wrong. "If we *confess* our sins, he is faithful and righteous to *forgive us our sins* and to cleanse us from all unrighteousness" (1 John 1:9, NASB, emphasis added).

When we admit that the act was wrong, and as we continue to turn away from evil, then we have forgiveness. The separation from God that we experience with sin is eliminated. God restores our relationship. That's a promise, even though we may not *feel* forgiven. Satan may frequently remind us of our past, but his whispering doubts cannot match God's promise of forgiveness.

Keep in mind, though, forgiveness doesn't eliminate all consequences. David received forgiveness, but the child still died, and violence plagued him the rest of his life. If I drink too much, hop on my motorcycle, take a ride into the countryside surrounding Temecula, run off the road into an orange tree and lose my leg, God will forgive me. Damage to our relationship from my disobedience will be overcome, but my leg probably won't grow back. Consequences remain.

AN EXCEPTION?

Now, if you played the smart reader and checked not only my biblical references but the context of them as well, you may see a possible problem here. Mark 3:28 gives the general principle that God forgives all sins, but verse 29 gives an exception we all wonder about: "But whoever blasphemes against the Holy Spirit will *never be forgiven*; he is guilty of an eternal sin" (emphasis added).

A *major* exception! Something for which we cannot be forgiven. Some squirm with this and water it down by saying that blaspheming the Holy Spirit means to reject the conviction of the Spirit, thereby rejecting Christ. This interpretation seems to do injustice to what Jesus said in the previous verse about the abundance of forgiveness.

I think Jesus goes much deeper. Jesus said all sins but this could be forgiven. By not defining it, we're left to wonder if we've done it—whatever "it" is!

A friend from Christian college days had grown up in church, left her relationship with God, came back, and then read the two following verses from Hebrews. She feared she'd done "it," and couldn't be forgiven. So with better faith than theology, she resolved she'd serve God in hell.

> It is *impossible* for those who have once been enlightened, who have tasted the heavenly gift, who have shared in the Holy Spirit, who have tasted the goodness of the word of God and the powers of the coming age, if they fall away, *to be brought back to repentance*, because to their loss they are crucifying the Son of God all over again and subjecting him to public disgrace (Hebrews 6:4-6, emphasis added).

If Jesus said blasphemy of the Spirit is the only unforgivable sin, and Hebrews uses another name but gives the same result, it seems logical that we must be talking about the same thing. (Christians disagree if the experience mentioned in the first verse of the Hebrews passage represents a genuine Christian or someone who just had a taste but didn't bite on the whole enchilada. Let's leave that alone as irrelevant for our discussion.)

What's the sign of having gone too far? According to Hebrews, being unable to repent. If a person can repent, the individual hasn't committed the unforgivable sin. Again from 1 John, confession brings forgiveness. If we experience a godly sorrow, a desire to move away from that sin, and agree with God that what we did was sin, then clearly we're receptive to the conviction of the Holy Spirit. Thus we haven't committed the unforgivable sin.

Little difference exists between people who *can't* repent and those who *don't* repent. In either case they have no forgiveness, so the operative concept is confessional repentance. God promises forgiveness to all who confess and repent.

ABUNDANT RESTORATION

Forgiveness eliminates the barrier between God and us that sin creates. Restoration works with the consequences, not by eliminating them, but by doing something even better: bringing good out of evil.

Fred dreamed of retiring at age forty. He loved leisure and viewed work as a necessary evil to pay the bills. On the job he worked just enough to do the main tasks, just enough to keep his position. But while Fred was in his late thirties, with little saved for retirement, the recession of the early 1990s hit. As the company downsized, Fred headed the list of those let go. His bosses needed people who worked hard, and he didn't match that description.

Fred enjoyed his time not working. He read a lot, improved his woodcarving skills, and relaxed—until his unemployment benefits ran out. His wife nagged him, so he started looking for another job. But his long time off and poor work ethic combined to make him nearly unemployable. They lost their house and moved into a small apartment. Stress grew.

Then he joined a men's group at his church studying Patrick Morley's book *The Man in the Mirror.* Fred read that work is a holy vocation, not a curse. He saw the love that some of the other men had for their jobs. He knew he'd never had that, and the realization of his laziness hit him like the proverbial 2 x 4 upside his head. He couldn't say a word during that meeting.

When he got home that night, he acknowledged his laziness to his wife, owned the results it had brought them, and begged her forgiveness. The next week he shared his experience with the other guys. One of them took a risk and hired him. The job didn't pay much, but it paid. It also gave Fred a sense of accomplishment he'd never felt before.

A few weeks later one of the guys had something to say: "Fred, I need to ask your forgiveness. I judged you from the beginning as a lazy slug. But God's been working on me. It's not just you; I'm critical toward everyone. Your being so open got me thinking, and God's been convicting me. You needed to change, and you told us that. Well, I need to change too, and I want to tell all of you that."

A marriage restored. Work integrity restored. Effective ministry restored. God's work of restoration acts to counteract the inherent damage of sin. He promised in Romans 8:28 "that *in all things* God *works for the good* of those who love him, who have been called according to his purpose" (emphasis added).

Since this verse is often misapplied, let's pick it apart to see what it does and does not say. We can extract four significant principles of restoration.

• *The extent of restoration: all things*

Very clearly, God can work in *all things*. That includes absolutely evil choices, apparently impossible situations, and all else. God doesn't actually work in every instance, for reasons we'll cover in a moment, but he can and wants to.

Grasping this can be a struggle. We see difficult situations we view as hopeless because we've seen similar circumstances end badly. Too many occasions in life demonstrate little of God's involvement, but the verse promises that God *can* work in *all* things.

• *The source of restoration: God*

We sometimes think "things work themselves out." Some translations even suggest this. The *New Revised Standard Version* says, "We know that all *things work together* for good ..." (emphasis added). Things don't always work out on their own. Left to themselves, "things" usually follow the principle of inertia: an object at rest or in motion tends to stay at rest or in motion unless acted upon by an outside force. God's intervention in Fred's situation changed his life.

This dimension of God's sovereignty amazes me. I firmly believe God has granted us free will, but a question comes up when I try to ponder how God works with the multiplied bad choices of billions of people and yet still works his will for good.

How does he do that? My only answer: He's God, and I'm not. And he works in all things.

• The purpose of restoration: good

When God works, he does so to bring good out of evil and to restore the harmony he desires for our lives. Obviously, that's good by his definition! God doesn't promise to work toward what *I* consider good.

Not long ago, while traveling to my cherished Sierra Nevada Mountains, the transmission in my Honda gave out just south of Lone Pine. I limped into town, found a reliable garage, and asked God to work for good. I knew the verse!

I had in mind God providing a new Jaguar XK8, either as a free loaner or as a free replacement. (Believe it or not, that didn't happen. I rented a car while they fixed mine, so I still got to fish, and that was good!) During a wait, the owner and I struck up a conversation. This was even better. He said he believed in God, and, that while Christianity worked for some people, if you were a good, sincere person, you'd go to heaven.

We had a fascinating discussion about relativity, absolute truth, and what the Bible says about each. Did I mention I'd just listened to a Josh McDowell radio broadcast on absolute truth? God works, doesn't he? Did Kevin make a commitment to personally accept Christ and absolute truth? Not then, but I went back up to the Sierras last week and dropped off that McDowell tape. God did use that difficult (and expensive) time. He worked for good, even though I didn't get the new Jag.

Sometimes the good God works for isn't visible to us—ever. That can be frustrating. We want to *see* the good both to give purpose to our lives and to expand our view of how God works. Still, I've seen God bring good from bad before, so I know I can trust him in the times I don't see his activity.

• The limits of restoration: our cooperation

We mentioned earlier that God limits the extent of his work. Actually, we limit his work. When we quote Romans 8:28, we typically use the first part: "And we know that in all things God works for good …" This incomplete version implies that

God always works, which doesn't always match reality, which makes us wonder if God told the truth.

We need the rest of the verse: "... God works for the good of *those who love him*, who have been *called according to his purpose*" (emphasis added). God promises to work for the good of those in a love relationship with him. Do we love other things more than God? Then God doesn't promise to work for good. He may, and he often does, but he doesn't promise. The next phrase explains why.

We must cooperate with God's purpose for us. Are we willing to allow God to do whatever he desires in us? Do we accept that activity as the most loving and the best? Then we free God to act like God. He won't overpower our will, so if we won't cooperate with his purposes, he may choose not to act. He may limit his promise to work for good by our degree of cooperation. Yes, sin damages us. And sometimes the consequences remain with us forever. But the truth is that God's forgiveness eliminates the barrier our sin creates, and God's restoration allows us to get back on track spiritually and be useful to him.

Live the Truth

How do we best incorporate the principles of forgiveness and restoration? Ironically, we only begin to balance the damage of sin when we come to grips with the reality of it.

ACKNOWLEDGE SIN'S DAMAGE

We've often referred to 1 John 1:9, a verse that shows how forgiveness flows as we accept the truth of our sin. Because sin damages people, we need to do our best to undo that, expressing a sincere concern for those we've damaged.

Probably the most hated day of the year is April 15. Tax day. The IRS Day of Reckoning. But as much as we dislike taxes, first-century Jews hated the tax collectors even more. The taxmen collaborated with the despised Roman government and frequently became wealthy from collecting more than what was required. Zacchaeus was a tax collector and a wealthy one at that. People identified him as a sinner. Just like those around him and like us. But also like us, Zacchaeus recognized his need for

God and that he had wronged people, and he wanted to make his relationships right. He told Jesus, "Look, Lord! Here and now I give half of my possessions to the poor, and *if I have cheated* anybody out of anything, I will *pay back* four times the amount" (Luke 19:8, emphasis added).

When we damage others, we need to make it right. Fred damaged his wife, his marriage, and their finances by his laziness. How did he make it right? Not just by saying he was sorry and wouldn't do it again. By acknowledging he'd wronged her. By working rigorously. He needed each of those pieces to rebuild the trust and intimacy he'd damaged.

Can we truly grieve over the damage we've brought and not try to make it right? I don't think so.

LEARN FROM PAST MISTAKES

We balance the damage of sin by not remaining vulnerable to that same sin. Jesus displayed amazing grace to the woman caught in adultery—he refused to condemn her—but we often miss his last command to her: "Go now and leave your life of sin" (John 8:11). Jesus wanted her to turn her back on her former way of life. The Bible doesn't tell us whether or not she obeyed, but I can give you an update on Fred. At this time, Fred has worked hard on the same job for over three years. He's earned some promotions, and he remains committed to doing his best both at work and at home.

Now, am I teaching perfectionism? Not at all! (Just go back to Lie 2.) But if we want to make up for the damage our sin brought, we need to move away from that sin. We need to make the solid inner decision that we don't want that sin and its damage in our lives. We choose to give less and less room to it. The Bible calls this repentance—turning away from our sin—a progressive victory over temptation.

MOVE BEYOND

More than just learning from our past sins, we need to become future oriented. We clearly identify our goal and move beyond the person we once were. Paul had this single-minded commitment to his future. Specifically, he refers to forgetting past accomplishments, but this principle applies to anything in our past that keeps us from moving into the future. That certainly includes our sins.

> I want to know Christ and the power of his resurrection and the fellowship of sharing in his sufferings, becoming like him in his death, and so, somehow, to attain to the resurrection from the dead. Not that I have already obtained all this, or have already been made perfect, but I press on to take hold of that for which Christ Jesus took hold of me. Brothers, I do not consider myself yet to have taken hold of it. But one thing I do: *Forgetting what is behind* and straining toward what is ahead, *I press on toward the goal* to win the prize for which God has called me heavenward in Christ Jesus (Philippians 3:10–14, emphasis added).

Paul "forgot" any past sins that kept him from being the kind of person who could reach his goal. He learned from them and moved beyond them. They weren't "him" any longer.

Paul demonstrated a straightforward progression that we can apply to our own lives. We need to

—acknowledge that our sins brought damage;

—do what we can to right the wrong;

—learn enough to avoid the sin in the future; and

—move on with our lives, always reaching toward God.

BASK IN RESTORATION

When we work this process, we can enjoy the fruit of restoration. Listen to Jesus' evaluation of Zacchaeus's commitment: "Today salvation has come to this house" (Luke 19:9). Salvation isn't only about an eternal destination. The word also refers to wholeness or to restoration to God's design. When we receive God's gift of salvation, we overcome the damage brought to us by our sin. We're not forever cursed with God's second best.

Even serious sins don't invalidate our ability to know and serve God. Serious sins like King David's: adultery with murder to cover it up. Despite his guilt and despite the damage, David responded to God's conviction and learned from it. In Acts 13:22 God evaluates David's spiritual condition: "I have found David son of Jesse *a man after my own heart*; he will do everything I want him to do" (emphasis added).

Is that your heart's cry—to be a man or woman after God's own heart? But have you sinned? Have you felt unqualified for God's best? Then remember the story of David. God offers forgiveness and restoration far more powerful than the guilt and damage of sin. And that's the truth.

Log the Truth

1. Think of one sin that brought significant damage to your life. What impact has it had on your closeness with God, your attitude toward yourself, or your relationships with others?

2. Think of a time that you sinned, damage resulted, and you dealt with it firmly. Has God used that to enhance your walk with him or your ministry? Describe that process.

3. What most troubles you about forgiveness?

4. What most encourages you about forgiveness?

5. Describe how you'll work with God for restoration in your life.

Lie 6

I'm Not Perfect, but Compared to Jim, I'm a Saint

The Truth about Comparisons

B lame it on the combination of junior high and slow development. As best as I can determine looking back, those two forces devastated my self-esteem. We took physical fitness tests in our first week, and I couldn't do a single acceptable push-up. While other boys exulted in their facial and underarm hair, I kept my arms at my sides when not wearing a shirt, hoping to hide the proof that puberty hadn't hit me yet. Body surfing at the beach made that particularly awkward. One seventh-grade student, Ed, exceeded six feet and shaved regularly. He had to, since a five o'clock shadow before the school day ended wasn't cool back then. I could only dream.

I felt out of place, like a loser. I don't recall having low self-esteem before those years, but seventh grade made it part of my identity. A part I despised and vowed to overcome. By the time high school came along, I had developed an excellent compensation strategy: comparison. I built characteristics with which I could carefully compete with others. If I came out ahead, that meant I was better. And if I was better, then certainly I had to be good. Simple deductions, really.

I did push-ups and sit-ups during TV commercials until, by the eleventh grade, I could outperform everyone in my PE class. My sprint speed matched that of a swift snail, but I discovered the key to distance running was an ability to endure pain. I could do that for the rewards of winning. As a senior I joined the varsity cross-country team, and we were undefeated in the league and placed third among southern California high schools.

I worked enough at studies to keep an A average and qualified for various honor societies. I joined the debate team and won several trophies. Even church became a competitive arena: I ran for president of our junior high and high school youth groups and won. But the biggest self-esteem boost came when I realized pretty girls found me attractive.

I discovered that if I was careful enough, I could consistently come out better than almost anyone. If I wasn't more athletic, then I turned to better grades. If grades didn't do the job, then I compared who had the best-looking girlfriend. If I didn't have the cutest girl, then I made sure I was a better Christian. And if I lost on all those, then I could always fall back on having the best personality. In my eyes, that was always a winner.

Self-esteem and comparison went hand in hand for me. I learned how to make competition work to my advantage. In the process, however, relationships frequently became competitive rather than supportive. I viewed people as rivals, not friends.

I dealt with many of those issues when I came to a genuine relationship with Christ, but the ingrained patterns continued even after I entered the ministry. My self-esteem soared if my church was larger than a friend's, or if it grew at a faster rate. Or if I considered myself to be a better teacher. Or … You get the picture.

I discovered that I had bought into a lie: We can determine our spiritual well being by comparing ourselves to others.

Identify the Lie

Too often, we Christians fall into the trap of evaluating ourselves in light of others. We like to think God grades on the curve: As long as we rate above half the people, we're above average and doing well. Why? First, comparing ourselves to others is relatively easy. We can be subjective and use opinion rather than hold ourselves to an objective standard. Second, we can shape the results. When we choose the comparison, we can give ourselves an A+ any time we want to!

A popular poem from the '60s titled "Desiderata" by Max Ehrmann had the line, "If you compare yourself with others, you may become vain or bitter, for always there will be greater and lesser persons than yourself." In my days of comparing to build self-worth, I consistently chose people or standards I thought I could beat. That tactic saved me hours of useless rationalizing.

A few years ago my wife, Sheila, shared a frustration with a particular habit of mine, and I rationalized both to myself and to her that I was probably better than the vast majority of husbands in that area. I know I'm not alone in responding this way. Many Christians justify their sins by saying they're not as bad as Jeff. Or Lori. Or Mom or Dad. We can practically build an assurance of our salvation by thinking we're more committed than the Christian next door.

Even "professional" Christians, such as pastors, evaluate their success or its lack by comparison. A group of us started new churches in southern California back in the mid '80s, and we occasionally went to conferences together. Keith's church had grown larger than any of ours both in numbers and in significant spiritual vitality, and we viewed him with a mixture of admiration and envy. We thought we'd be successful if we could just grow our churches (with God's help, of course!) to the size of Keith's.

At one of those conferences, the founding pastor of a mega church shared his secrets of success. Afterward we debriefed over slices of apple pie, and Keith's discouragement poured forth. "You know, guys, this is so frustrating. I feel like such a failure compared to these speakers."

We had already faced the same phenomenon with Keith, so we were surprised to find he now experienced it on our side of the fence. Funny, isn't it, how we can always come out better or worse, depending on whom we compare ourselves to?

Comparison isn't limited to contemporary believers. I suspect that failing the comparison game added to the depth of temptation faced by Adam and Eve. What was Satan's greatest ploy? "Do this, and you'll be like God" (Genesis 3:5). They'd seen just how great God is, and they wanted to be like him. They failed the comparison test.

Saul, the first king of Israel, failed when compared to David, and the failure ate at him like a worm in an apple. Finally he couldn't stand himself and schemed to have David killed (1 Samuel 18:1-12; 19).

The apostles repeatedly quarreled over who was greatest, and, of course, the only way to determine the greatest is by comparison. Jesus knew of their ambition and didn't approve.

> They came to Capernaum. When he was in the house, he asked them, "What were you arguing about on the road?" But they kept quiet because on the way they had argued about who was the greatest. Sitting down, Jesus called the Twelve and said, "If anyone wants to be first, he must be the very last, and the servant of all" (Mark 9:33-35).

The early church frequently demonstrated sacrificial giving, perhaps with Barnabas as the greatest example, as told in Acts 4:34-5:11. Barnabas sold some property and gave it to the church. A husband and wife knew their reputation didn't compare well to Barnabas, but they wanted it to. So they likewise sold some property and gave *part* of it to the church, which was entirely okay. But to build their reputation, they said they gave it all. They wanted to compare well to Barnabas, but without the sacrifice. Comparisons killed them. Literally.

Have you seen this tendency in your life? In the lives of other believers? We've all been trapped by this lie more than once. We've seen the damage that the lie brings to our lives. It's time to discover the truth.

Learn the Truth

Not only must we identify how this lie has affected us, we need to move into the arena of truth. Very simply, we can only gauge our spiritual progress by using God's objective standards. Basing our godliness on how we stack up against other Christians only results in a false satisfaction. As a result, we stop growing spiritually, thinking we've arrived when we haven't. When we compare ourselves to what God desires for us, however, we can then *be* what God desires for us.

Obviously, this single chapter can't mention and evaluate all of God's standards! Let's look at five basic principles that can guide our search for truth in the arena of comparisons.

WE AVOID COMPARISONS

Galatians 6:4-5 provides the foundational truth: "Each one should test his own actions. Then he can take pride in himself, without comparing himself to somebody else, for each one should carry his own load."

Paul makes it clear that we cannot evaluate how we're doing by comparing ourselves to others. The truth is, we need to avoid comparisons. Why? The last phrase in that passage yields the next principle.

WE ACCEPT INDIVIDUAL RESPONSIBILITY

When we comprehend the implication of "each one should carry his own load," then we know that we must be responsible for our own lives. We need to own our choices and not let ourselves off the hook because we're not as bad as another. If we're bad, we're bad! We cannot justify ourselves because we do better than someone else.

WE EXAMINE OURSELVES

If we can't justify ourselves by comparing, and we are responsible for our own decisions, then it makes sense that we should ruthlessly look at our own lives rather than focusing on others and how we match up to them. Go back to another phrase in Galatians: "Each one should test his own actions."

We don't test others to see if they make the grade. We don't test others to see if they make us look good. We check out our own lives. I hate to say this, and I hate even more to do it, but brutal self-examination should be a regular part of our lives. And, God graciously provides a memory aid for that!

The first-century church met for worship each week on Sunday, in honor of the Lord's resurrection. And each week they observed communion as part of worship. Acts 20:7 says, "On the first day of the week we came together to break bread. Paul spoke to the people …"

It seems that the primary purpose and function of their weekly worship was to break bread, or to celebrate the Lord's Supper. They remembered Jesus' death, burial, and resurrection that brought the forgiveness of our sins. Each week. At each worship event. Why did Communion play such a vital part of their worship? Look what the apostle Paul instructed them to do as part of the Lord's Supper.

> For whenever you eat this bread and drink this cup, you proclaim the Lord's death until he comes. Therefore, whoever eats the bread or drinks the cup of the Lord in an unworthy manner will be guilty of sinning against the body and blood of the Lord. *A man ought to examine himself before he eats of the bread and drinks of the cup.* For anyone who eats and drinks without recognizing the body of the Lord eats and drinks judgment on himself. That is why many among you are weak and sick, and a number of you have fallen asleep. But if we judged ourselves, we would not come under judgment (1 Corinthians 11:26–31, emphasis added).

God graciously provides an opportunity to examine ourselves. We do that when we use God's standards to evaluate our attitudes and actions. Not in comparison to others, but in comparison to Jesus, who gave his life for us.

WE USE GOD'S STANDARDS

To accurately examine ourselves, we need to determine which standards and values we use. I can't overemphasize the importance of this.

In my early days, when I picked the standards of comparison, I did well! When I carefully chose whom to compare myself to, I could beat the standard. My standards were effective in that they accomplished what I wanted them to, but they were completely invalid. Galatians 6:4 makes that clear. True standards don't come from comparing ourselves to others.

Likewise, true standards don't come from choosing our own values. Our tendency toward this practice reflects our culture's current value of relativism, that no values are absolute, that each individual can choose his own (see the author's book with David Timms, *Just Leave God Out of It and Other Cultural Compromises We Make* for a deeper examination of relativism).

The apostle Paul shows the inadequacy of both choosing standards of comparison and personal values in 2 Corinthians 10:12: "We do not dare to classify or compare ourselves with some who commend themselves. When they measure themselves by themselves and compare themselves with themselves, they are not wise."

First, Paul avoided comparing himself to others. Second, he recommended against "measuring themselves against themselves." Who can say whether one person's set of values is better or worse than another's? Who can determine whether I should compare myself to this person or that person? If we choose either the standard or the object of comparison, we determine the results (and we usually slant them in our favor!).

We don't receive praise from God for meeting our own standards or for doing "better" than others. Move down six verses to 2 Corinthians 10:18: "For it is not the one who commends himself who is approved, but the one whom the Lord commends."

When will God commend us? When we *follow his standards*, as given in his Word. Paul makes that clear in 2 Timothy 3:16–17: "All Scripture is God-breathed and is useful for teaching, rebuking, correcting and training in righteousness, so that the man of God may be thoroughly equipped for every good work."

That means we find all we need to build valid spiritual self-worth in the Bible. Absolute evaluative standards can be found there. God gives commands. He provides direction. He gives behavioral standards we can use to gauge our spiritual maturity. Let's consider just one scriptural passage that affirms that.

> Blessed are they whose ways are blameless, who walk according to the law of the LORD. Blessed are they who keep his statutes and seek him with all their heart. They do nothing wrong; they walk in his ways. You have laid down precepts that are to be fully obeyed. Oh, that my ways were steadfast in obeying your decrees! (Psalm 119:1-5).

WE BUILD BIBLICAL PRIDE

When we follow God's pattern, we can then take biblical pride in our lives. We are pleased because God is pleased. Let's not discount this! Some Christians believe that all forms of pride are sinful. We've already seen that pride arising from comparing ourselves to others is invalid. But we can determine our spiritual state—and build spiritual esteem and pride—when we compare ourselves to the standards God has given.

Are we closer to him now than a year ago? Do we experience progressive victory over difficult temptations? Do we stretch ourselves by attempting new ministries? Has our character become more Christlike?

If we can answer those questions positively, then we can take good and valid spiritual pride in who we have become in Christ. Let me suggest we need this! Good pride comes not from comparing ourselves to others, but by following God and his standards. We've cooperated with God, and that's good.

Live the Truth

Let's look at three specific areas in which we need to carefully avoid comparisons.

WE DON'T COMPARE OUR SALVATION

First, we don't compare ourselves to others to determine if we're saved. A recent survey indicated that 80 percent of Americans think they're above average spiritually. They believe they're going to heaven, that they're good enough to stay out of hell. Obviously, 80 percent of people can't be above average—just do the math!

Most Americans believe we make heaven's entrance requirements if we're good enough. And for many of us, "good enough" means better than most. By our own judgment. Many folks believe they're better than the next-door neighbor, who beats his dog. They may beat their kids, but the dog is innocent and the kids aren't. So they're okay. Sure, they get mad at overspending in the government, and maybe they cheat a little on their taxes because of that, but they certainly don't go overboard like Timothy McVeigh. So they're okay.

We may not be perfect, but compared to Jim we're a saint. And saints go to heaven, right? Wrong. At least, not people who define themselves as saints because they're "good." The question is not "am I good enough?" The question is, what are God's entrance standards? Read the Ephesians 2:8–9: "God saved you by his special favor when you believed. And you can't take credit for this; it is a gift from God. Salvation is not a reward for the good things we have done, so none of us can boast about it" (NLT).

We live in the truth when we base our salvation on believing in Christ as our Lord and Savior, not on being good. Do you remember the classic scene in the movie *The Fugitive*, when Tommy Lee Jones, playing a federal agent, traps Harrison Ford at the end of a tunnel? Ford proclaims his innocence, and Lee responds, "I don't care."

Why didn't Jones care? He wasn't the judge or jury. His job was to bring Ford back. Let me suggest that in regard to our salvation, when we try to tell God how good we are, he replies, "I don't care."

Why? Because our goodness has nothing to do with being saved. Absolutely nothing. Now, it has much to do with how we live as Christians. Once we commit to God, our behavior certainly matters. But since God doesn't grade our goodness on the curve for salvation, we can't compare our level of goodness to others' for salvation.

WE DON'T COMPARE OUR MATURITY

The second step in living this out means we don't determine our level of spiritual maturity in comparison to others. We face the same problem we mentioned earlier: we can either gain false confidence, or false discouragement when we look at those who "exceed" or "don't match" where we are spiritually. But most significantly, our evaluations are not based on the entire truth.

I've made that mistake more than once, but never more clearly as when I interviewed for a position as associate minister at the Lawndale Christian Church. The job was to oversee the entire youth ministry and to work directly with the college/career group. I was relieved when I got through what I thought would be the most difficult stage: talking with the pastor and his wife. Next up was a group interview with the elders and all the adult youth workers, which I thought would be a breeze.

I was wrong. I got grilled like a cheap steak. One elder, a vice president for a major oil company and a worker with the college group, asked all the tough questions—where I stood on salvation, charismatic issues, dating college students, beliefs on Christians drinking alcohol, and more. Worse yet, each of my answers prompted deeper questions. Don was a bulldog. He started off on a course of questions and wouldn't give up.

I began to wonder if I wanted to work with a person so crucial to the ministry, but seemingly so critical in spirit. Silently, I even questioned his spiritual maturity. But before I could say no to the job, I got a chance to know Don—and not just on the surface. He loved the church and young people. He had dedicated his life to serving God. He wanted to be sure the church called the right person, not just someone who seemed okay on the surface. So he probed. Deep. He asked the difficult questions.

I discovered that my initial reading of Don was absolutely wrong. He wasn't critical; he cared. He wasn't a bulldog; he thought carefully about the depth of an issue. He possessed great spiritual maturity, far more than I had. Don became a great supporter and coworker with the college group because he went below surface appearances. I also had to go beyond my initial evaluation of him. Our true spiritual condition could only be seen when we looked past first impressions, and both of us had to take time to see the heart of the other.

When we compare our level of spiritual maturity to another person's, we ignore where that person started. We don't know their heart and motives. Perhaps they did the wrong act out of absolutely sinful motives. Or maybe their motives were excellent, but their wisdom didn't measure up. Maybe they made a wise decision based on great motives, but factors outside their control changed what happened.

Each of those three scenarios would cause us to evaluate them differently. But we frequently can't determine which of the three happened. We get stuck looking at outward appearances, and that inaccurate perception will change how we compare to others.

In the first century, the Pharisees seemed to be the high-point of spiritual maturity. They were educated, committed, and sacrificial—on the outside. But look at how Jesus evaluated where they really were.

> "Woe to you, teachers of the law and Pharisees, you hypocrites! You are like whitewashed tombs, which look beautiful on the outside but on the inside are full of dead men's bones and everything unclean. In the same way, on the outside you appear to people as righteous but on the inside you are full of hypocrisy and wickedness" (Matthew 23:27–28).

They looked great spiritually to many people who only saw their outward acts. Inwardly sin filled their hearts. Were they truly as spiritually mature as they seemed? Not at all.

We need to determine our spiritual maturity based on how far *we've* come. We compare our lives to biblical standards. And we waste no time evaluating how spiritually mature we are by comparing.

WE DON'T COMPARE OUR MINISTRY

Have you heard the phrase "preacher count"? Preacher count doubles the size of what a layperson would count! It comes from pastors' tendencies to exaggerate to make their ministries look better. I'll never forget an elder who accused me of preacher count.

I reported our Easter attendance at an elders' meeting, and one person took immediate offense. "Tim, I just don't think that's possible. I didn't come anywhere close to that when I estimated the worship service." I was guilty by reputation. Actually, I didn't make the count. A deacon who wasn't particularly a supporter had done it. But Henry still thought I'd exaggerated.

Many of us tend to compare the quality of our ministries to affirm what we do. When pastors meet, not much time passes before one asks, "What are you running nowadays?" He's not inquiring about your time running the mile! Rather, he wants to know your church's attendance, so both you and he can be placed in the proper pecking order of importance. One friend consistently answers, "Oh, we're just a bit under a thousand." In truth, his church averages about fifty in worship attendance. Technically, he's right: attendance is certainly under a thousand!

Members do the same in bragging about the size of their churches. Or how important their personal ministry is, or its growth, or how much responsibility they have. Of course, we're subtle about it, but we still do it. Christians aren't perfect, but we know how to spin our words to make ourselves look as close as possible.

That tendency of comparing ministries started early on with the apostles. Jesus gave Peter an important ministry assignment, and he became the leader of the Jerusalem church. But he couldn't stop comparing himself to John.

> Peter turned and saw that the disciple whom Jesus loved was following them. (This was the one who had leaned back against Jesus at the supper and had said, "Lord, who is going to betray you?") When Peter saw him, he asked, "Lord, what about him?" Jesus answered, "If I want him to remain alive until I return, what is that to you? You must follow me" (John 21:20–22).

Peter got caught up comparing his ministry to John's. How did Jesus respond? If I can paraphrase, he said, "Peter, do your job. Forget his job; do what I told you to do." Or, "Do your ministry. Don't compare.

Our chapter on ministry will explore this in more depth and will provide more reasons to not compare. But in the meantime, we need to avoid the trap of thinking that our ministry gains affirmation when we compare it to what others are doing.

WE CAN COMPARE WHEN ...

Can we ever compare ourselves to others? Yes, if we're careful. I believe that most of us need concrete examples of the Christian life. The writer of Hebrews knew that well when he said, "Remember your leaders, who spoke the word of God to you. Consider the outcome of their way of life and *imitate their faith*" (13:7, emphasis added).

We can wisely pick out people who have reached a good level of spiritual growth and use them as models. Jesus with flesh on, so to speak. Not blindly, not doing all they do exactly the same way they do it. But see how they handle situations. Explore how they've grown. Get inside their minds and spirit, and use those lessons to avoid making mistakes on your own.

We can even learn from negative examples. I had the good fortune to have outstanding teachers as I worked my way through school, and I never thought I could match the standards they set for being a great teacher. Until I met Mr. Smith in my senior year of high school. He did well as an athletic coach, but he failed as a teacher. With all the arrogance of teen years, I thought, "I can do that better than he does." Several years later I did teach at a secondary school.

I also had a college professor who was less than terrific, and again I thought, "I can do that better than he does." I now teach at a Christian university.

What's the balance? We don't seek self-worth through comparisons. We don't gain assurance of salvation or of the importance of our ministries through comparisons. But we can validly evaluate how we compare as a way to motivate ourselves to a higher level of thinking or behaving.

No, I'm not perfect. But compared to Jim, I'm still Tim. That's okay, and that's the truth!

Log the Truth

1. In what ways have you compared yourself to others? How did those comparisons affect your actions and your view of yourself?

2. What does Galatians 6:4–5 say to you? ("Each one should test his own actions. Then he can take pride in himself, without comparing himself to somebody else, for each one should carry his own load.")

3. How does knowing that God saves you by grace rather than by being good change your view of yourself?

4. Have you initially judged another person as spiritually immature, and later discovered you were wrong? Describe what happened.

5. Has measuring the "success" of your ministry with others hurt or helped you? Why?

Lie 7

I Married the Wrong Person

The Truth about God's Will

Wes captivated his nationwide television audience as he told his life story. His father had died when Wes was still young, and the family frequently struggled. Then, at fourteen he heard the message of Jesus and accepted Christ. Even though he'd never even heard a sermon, he knew God had a plan for his life: He was to preach. No doubt existed in his young mind.

He entered the university and earned several theological degrees. A church in the South called him as pastor, and he led it in significant growth. Next, God orchestrated a series of moves that astounded the young preacher. Opportunities for both television and radio exposure exploded. He now teaches on over 200 television and 400 radio stations, and his ministry reaches every nation on earth.

He has no doubt that God crafted this plan for his life. That conviction he felt at fourteen has never faded. God had a plan for Wes and worked the plan. Wes's job was to be faithful to God's will for him.

Then Wes took it a step further. He believes God has made plans for each Christian, that God scripts a life for each of us that will advance his mission. I heard the same message while growing up: God had a plan for my life. He'd even picked out the ideal wife! However, I honestly feared she might live in China, and I'd never even meet her.

Doesn't the idea of God having a plan for us sound exciting? God, who truly knows all and knows best, sets the direction for our lives. We don't have to make those painful decisions. We just follow. The very best path for our lives has already been planned out.

Many of us don't seem to experience that level of guidance, however. I know I've missed the boat more than once, even when I sincerely and passionately sought God. Sometimes God has led like a pillar of fire in the night sky. Other times all I see is darkness. Perhaps you've experienced the same.

What's the problem? When we expect God to plan every detail of our lives, we fall prey to a lie—a lie that possesses much truth but has just enough inaccuracy to bring problems.

Identify the Lie

What's the lie? God has one specific will for our lives. Or, God crafts one particular path for each believer. Before we get too far down this road, let's examine the biblical evidence that indicates this belief has a great deal of truth behind it. We can find abundant examples of God's choosing a path for a person, as well as individual verses that seem to support that idea.

GOD'S PLAN FOR MOSES

Moses failed after forty years of being a royal. He believed he could use his position for God, but he flopped miserably and got run out of the country. He spent the next forty years working as a lowly shepherd, almost hidden in the wilderness. At this point, we see little of God's hand on him.

But in Exodus 3–4, God appears and says that he has a very specific plan to use Moses to free his people from slavery. Moses responds, "God, I don't mean to be disrespectful, but I think you have the wrong guy. Now, my brother Aaron, he's topnotch. Talk to him about this plan of yours."

God deals with Moses's attempt to defer to Aaron by saying, "Yahweh wants you." Moses uses four specific excuses, and God responds to each.

Finally, running out of reasons, Moses simply blurts out, "O Lord, please send someone else to do it."

God had a plan for Moses, Moses tried to squirm out of it, and God relentlessly told Moses, "I want you. Specifically." God clearly had a plan for the man Moses, and he wasn't about to let Moses escape that.

GOD'S PLAN FOR PAUL

Look in the New Testament at a rabid Christian-hater named Saul. He supported the killing of the first martyr, Stephen, and then took it further. "But Saul began to destroy the church. Going from house to house, he dragged off men and women and put them in prison" (Acts 8:3).

Saul's actions certainly didn't match any plan God might have had for him. But God didn't give up on recruiting Paul to serve him. In Acts 9, as Saul traveled to Damascus to continue his work, a brilliant light flashed about him and his companions, a loud voice thundered, and the group with Saul was thrown to the ground. Saul himself was blinded by the light.

Jesus spoke to him and gave some very specific instructions about what to do. Later, with his name changed to Paul, he retold the story with a fascinating twist. "We all fell to the ground, and I heard a voice saying to me in Aramaic, 'Saul, Saul, why do you persecute me? It is hard for you to kick against the goads'" (Acts 26:14).

Apparently, Jesus had been trying to get Saul's attention for some time, but he had resisted. God wanted Saul. He had a clear plan for him, and not even Saul trying to destroy the church would change God's mind.

GOD'S PLAN FOR GOD'S PEOPLE

Yes, God worked like that with Moses and Saul, but those examples may not serve as a general pattern. Does God do the same with us? Let's explore Jeremiah 29:11, a verse frequently used to promise that God will reveal his one-and-only will for our lives.

"For I know the plans I have for you," declares the LORD, "plans to prosper you and not to harm you, plans to give you hope and a future."

Awesome! God has plans for us. Good plans. A future with hope and prosperity. This verse is a clear indication that God both cares for us and provides a comforting plan for our lives. Isn't it?

Many churches teach a method of interpreting the Bible that states, "Every promise in the book is mine; every chapter, every verse, every line." If that is true, then we can claim the promise of Jeremiah, and Moses and Paul provide examples of how God works in our lives.

But is this true?

Can we really claim all biblical promises for our benefit? Does each story of how God worked with an individual mean that God will work like that with us? Although what we've explored so far is biblical, it certainly doesn't include the entirety of the scriptural testimony on this issue of God's will. Yes, it's true; but no, it's not complete.

Can we claim Moses's experience as normative for us? Not unless God speaks directly to us through a bush that burns but not up. Can we use Paul's example as a pattern that God pursues us with a specific plan for our lives? Not unless we, like Paul, experience thunder, a literally blinding light, and a clear voice speaking to us. Deeper yet, to accurately interpret the Bible, we can't assume that the experience of each Bible character provides a pattern for us.

Let me explain that, because we come close to slippery ground when we start to say some parts of the Bible don't apply to all believers. We can easily rule out *any* passage we don't particularly like, and that's dangerous. But not all passages *do* apply, so how can we tell the difference?

Two different grids help determine what applies. First, passages tend to be normative, narrative, or problematic. *Normative* passages generally apply to all in the group addressed, it's the normal way we follow God. General commands fit here, such as Jesus telling us to remember him in communion (1 Corinthians 11:25). *Narrative passages* describe what happened, but not necessarily as a command. The early church seemed to take communion each week in worship, but we're not commanded to do that. We just have their example (Acts 20:7). *Problematic* passages express specific solutions to specific problems, and tend to not apply beyond the problem, such as how the church in Corinth abused communion, and Paul gave specific remedies (1 Corinthians 11:17-22).

Narrative passages don't automatically provide a command or pattern for us. Not unless we're willing to follow Judas's example of how to deal with the guilt that follows sin, or even to follow David's example of how to raise our children. Perhaps the experiences of Moses and Paul belonged only to Moses and Paul and show us, not a blueprint for our lives, but how God worked with two specific people, in a specific time and place, for a specific purpose.

A second grid breaks down various commands into moral, ceremonial, or wisdom. Moral commands flow from the unchanging moral character of God, and don't change. The Old Covenant command to avoid adultery flows from God's faithfulness and applies to all. Ceremonial commands flow from the specific covenant a person lives under. For instance, the sacrificial system applied to the nation of Israel, but not to the church. Jesus' sacrifice fulfilled that; the terms of the covenant have changed.

Wisdom commands deal with practical advice, a good way to live, but without moral implications. God commanded that armies build trench latrines and cover their waste (Deuteronomy 23:12-13). Did that bring them closer to God? No, it brought them closer to good health!

Instead of simply assuming every individual biblical narrative is a pattern, we need to ask a few key questions about a given passage:

- When was it written?
- What is the context?
- Who is it addressed to?
- Why was it written?

•Is there any indication this passage applies to other individuals or groups?

Let's apply those questions to Jeremiah.

When was it written, and what was the context? We find a clue in Jeremiah 29:4: "This is what the LORD Almighty, the God of Israel, says to all those I carried into exile from Jerusalem to Babylon ..."

God promised a great future to the people of Israel during their captivity in Babylon. He directed this promise to the nation of Israel. Let's go a step further to verse 10: "This is what the Lord says: 'When seventy years are completed for Babylon, I will come to you and fulfill my gracious promise to bring you back to this place.'"

Only after verse 10 comes the promise that God has a plan, but what does the context tell us about that promise? God promised *the nation of Israel*, captive in Babylon, that he would bring them back to the land of Israel and do good things for them. Doesn't that anchor the promise to 597 B.C.? Does anything in that promise indicate that Christians today are included? I can't find it.

I don't want to say that God never has plans for his people! But that verse doesn't promise plans for all Christians. We do a great injustice to God's Word when we try to make it say things it doesn't say on its own.

The Danger Zone

For the sake of discussion, assume we agree that neither narrative examples—like Moses and Paul—nor promises like Jeremiah 29:11 provide proof of God having a detailed plan for the lives of each Christian. So why is this important?

Go back to the story of Wes with whom we opened this chapter. I've been a Christian pretty much my whole life. While I've certainly sensed God's leading—and sometimes very strongly—I've never had the conviction Wes did that God has his life planned out. And I have felt inadequate and unspiritual because of that. Why couldn't *I* hear God's voice so clearly? Was I too insignificant for God to have a plan? Or even worse, what if I missed God's plan? Am I destined for less than God's best?

Not so much from God's chosen wife living in China, but should I have entered the ministry earlier in life? Should I have not done so? Should I have taken each pastoral post I did?

From talking to Christians and seekers for several decades, I've found most have had similar experiences. We're apt to struggle in trying to find God's will. We fear we've "missed it." We dread settling for God's second best (or third, fourth, or worse) because we made a decision that didn't match God's will for us. And we're afraid once we make a bad decision, we can't ever get back on track.

Expectations that cannot be met breed frustration. So if we expect God to have a specific and detailed will for our lives, and we can't find it, we grow discouraged. We're tempted to give up. So, when it comes to God's will for us, what's the truth?

Learn the Truth

Yes, God does have a will for us. Knowing what we can rightfully expect will decrease discouragement and increase living in God's will.

Some years ago I went through the entire Bible and found each verse that talked about God's will. I discovered that God's will fit into two categories: God's will in general and God's will in specifics. The first one we can always know without any doubt. The other tends to be a little more flexible and difficult to determine.

GOD'S WILL IN GENERAL

Every passage I found that clearly said "this is God's will with no doubt" fit into two categories. Both are God's will for every person on earth.

First, God wills that every person come to a relationship with his Son Jesus as Savior and Lord. "This is good, and pleases God our Savior, who *wants all men to be saved* and to come to a knowledge of the truth" (1 Timothy 2:3-4, emphasis added). God wants each person to freely choose to become a follower of Jesus. Does that always happen? Of course not. God's will isn't always done. Many reject Jesus, as he himself said they would in Matthew 7:13-14: "Enter through the narrow gate. For wide is the gate and broad is the road that leads to destruction, and many enter through it. But small is the gate and narrow the road that leads to life, and only a few find it."

Second, God wills that all those who accept Jesus develop in their faith, that they enter a process of transformation. First Thessalonians 4:3-6 tells us:

> It is *God's will that you should be sanctified*: that you should avoid sexual immorality; that each of you should learn to control his own body in a way that is holy and honorable, not in passionate lust like the heathen, who do not know God; and that in this matter no one should wrong his brother or take advantage of him (emphasis added).

God wills that Christians be sanctified. Pay close attention to the grammatical structure used in the NIV. A colon follows "sanctified" in the text, meaning that what follows the colon describes our role in sanctification: that we avoid sexual immorality, that we control our bodies, that we not wrong others.

The word "sanctification" itself means that we set our lives apart for God, that we use them as he desires, that we grow in spiritual maturity. If we're growing in Christ, we're in God's will. If we're not growing, we're not in God's will.

Again, even God's general will doesn't always occur! Many Christians get stuck in a spiritual kindergarten, remaining baby believers. But God wills that we grow.

Every time I found a Bible passage that clearly linked God's will and all people, it matched one of these two issues—being saved or being sanctified. I found no verse that said God has a will for each and every Christian outside salvation and sanctification.

But what about Wes? Could he have been right, that God had a specific path for him? Absolutely. You see, God does care deeply about the details of our lives. Now, how does his will fit into those details?

GOD'S WILL IN SPECIFICS

I found no passage that indicates God has a comprehensive plan and direction for each individual Christian. He did for some individuals, as we saw with Moses and Paul. We learned, however, that narrative passages don't necessarily provide commands that compel each Christian to have exactly the same experiences as other believers. Even though both Paul and Moses resisted God's will for them, God quite firmly insisted on their obedience. Yet, as we'll discover a little later in this section, even within general direction God gives great freedom on specifics.

• Experiencing Direction

Most followers of Jesus have experienced times when God clearly gave us direction on a specific course of behavior. Sometimes we ask for that direction, other times God just gives it because he wants to. Several decades ago, a Christian mission group asked me to lead a month-long mission trip to a small mountain village outside Taos, New Mexico. I was then teaching at a Christian junior high and barely getting paid for it, certainly not enough to accumulate extra for a trip.

I wanted to go, however, so I asked God to provide the $400 the trip would cost. I scraped and saved and finally gathered the money.

Shortly thereafter, my favorite aunt from Tennessee asked my sister and me to come out and visit with her before cancer took her life. I couldn't say no, but the airfare was $400, so my savings for the mission trip was gone. We had a marvelous time together as family gathered. I truly didn't regret the decision, but still I yearned to make the trip.

On the last day of my visit, we all met with Aunt Gray in her hospital room. Hugs and tears flowed, and then she spoke. "Tim and Jane, I can't tell you how God has blessed me with seeing you two again. I know it's not much, but I'd like to leave you each $500 in my will—just as a sign of my love and appreciation for you."

God clearly indicated he wanted me on that mission trip, which, by the way, led to a series of events that completely changed the direction of my life. God had a will for me, and he made that clear.

Proverbs 16:9 offers us great assurance:"In his heart a man plans his course, but the LORD determines his steps." We make our plans, we ponder, we get advice, we pray, and we make our decisions. All the while God works to guide our steps. He has a will for us in many situations—situations that don't directly flow from being saved or from being sanctified.

Sometimes, God clearly wants us to get direction from him on specifics of life. But not always!

• *Experiencing Freedom*

Remember how God had a clear plan for the life of Paul? God wanted Paul to take the great news of Jesus to the non-Jewish world. And, within that context, God sometimes gave very specific directions. Let's explore 2 Corinthians 2:12–14 just one verse at a time.

"Now when I went to Troas to preach the gospel of Christ and found that *the Lord had opened a door for me* ..." (v. 12, emphasis added). Paul loved to preach the gospel, to tell about Jesus. He was passionate to reach non-Jews, God made it possible for him to do both. We don't know how the door opened, but Paul had no doubt that God directed him.

How did Paul react to God's direction? He went the other way! "I still had no peace of mind, because I did not find my brother Titus there. So I said good-by to them and *went on to Macedonia*" (v. 13, emphasis added).

God clearly showed where he wanted Paul to go, and Paul went the opposite direction. He ignored God's direction. The first time I read this, I expected the next verse to tell about a lightning bolt that blasted Paul out of existence! I didn't think Paul would get away with ignoring God's direction.

God was gracious, though. Read verse 14. "But thanks be to God, who *always leads us in triumphal procession* in Christ and through us spreads everywhere the fragrance of the knowledge of him" (emphasis added).

Get that order: God gives direction; Paul *chooses* to go the opposite direction; God still leads in triumph. What lesson does God guide us into? We have great freedom in choosing the course of our lives, the specifics of our lives. Sometimes God *has* a specific course for our lives, and he lets us know that, as he did with Moses and Paul. Sometimes he *allows us to choose* our basic direction.

Sometimes *God has a will for a specific act or event*, and he lets us know that. Sometimes he'll *give us his preference*, as he did with Paul at Troas, and allow us to choose another path. But he's always with us, always leading, always maintaining a fine tension between his will and our choosing.

Live the Truth

Rather than being robots that blindly follow their master, God wants us to learn how to discern his will, his direction, and his heart, so we can make godly decisions. Our problems don't come when God clearly reveals his will for us. At that point we just need to follow! Our difficulty comes when we face a spiritual decision and don't have a clue about what God wants us to do. Let me suggest a five-step process to determine God's will for us.

1. Pray

When we're facing a decision that seems impossible to make, we pray. We need to ask God for wisdom and for direction. We ask for our own openness to hear what God might lead us into and for a willingness to go there, regardless of the cost. Praying about a decision helps align us with God, to be both more sensitive and more willing.

I don't hesitate to tell God of my preferences, either! "God, if it's okay with you, please open the doors so we can move to Hawaii. I think I'd like that. But God, open and close doors to lead me where you most want me to go. I'll accept whatever you direct."

Prayer works. Not so much because God tells us out loud during the prayer what his will is, but because prayer helps us to desire that first of all. I've noticed doors open or close much more clearly after I acknowledge my preferences and then defer to God's will!

2. SEARCH THE SCRIPTURES

God usually reveals his will in his Word. Do we want to know how to be sanctified? Then we get to know God's Word. Do we face a decision with spiritual implications and don't quite know what God desires? Then we study that topic in Scripture, thoroughly exploring all the verses on that subject. We also look for general principles that touch on that subject from which we can draw some practical applications.

3. SEEK GODLY ADVICE

We talk to mature Christians who've gone through a situation similar to the one we face. Sometimes this can be a struggle, but we can expand our wisdom when we're willing to learn from others, at least according to Proverbs 19:20: "Listen to advice and accept instruction, and in the end you will be wise."

I encourage you to build a group of advisors. Identify people with a variety of experiences and expertise to whom you can go for advice. Make sure they're not just friends, but those who have lived the Christian life with some success over a period of time. Then when you face a decision, check out God's Word, learn what you can, and get input from your advisors.

4. KNOW GOD'S HEART

With some decisions, we search the Scriptures and just can't find a specific reference or a principle that applies. We want to do God's will, but what is it? Hebrews 5:13–6:2 encourages us to get to know God more deeply so that we *can* discern his will.

> Anyone who lives on milk, being still an infant, is not acquainted with the teaching about righteousness. But solid food is for the mature, who by constant use have trained themselves to distinguish good from evil. Therefore let us leave the elementary teachings about Christ and go

on to maturity, not laying again the foundation
of repentance from acts that lead to death, and
of faith in God, instruction about baptisms, the
laying on of hands, the resurrection of the dead,
and eternal judgment.

Our Christian life begins with learning the basics: faith, repentance, baptism, spiritual gifts, and end times. We progress in learning to distinguish between good and evil. We learn which option would best express the character of God. Or, we start to sense what might be God's heart in a matter. Asking the popular question, "What would Jesus do?" can be both a help and a hindrance. We can easily put our desires into determining what Jesus would do, but we can also move beyond our desires and get to know God's heart. We can learn to let his character and values be clear to us.

Getting to know God more deeply requires constant practice and training—it's a lifelong process.

5. Decide

We must be careful to wait until we've done the first four steps or until we have a clear answer at one point before we make a *tentative decision*. James 4:13–17 explains what I mean.

Now listen, you who say, "Today or tomorrow
we will go to this or that city, spend a year there,
carry on business and make money." Why, you do
not even know what will happen tomorrow.
What is your life? You are a mist that appears for
a little while and then vanishes. Instead, you
ought to say, "*If it is the Lord's will*, we will live
and do this or that." As it is, you boast and brag.
All such boasting is evil (emphasis added).

God gives us great freedom to participate in determining his will for us! First, we don't decide on our own that we *will* do something. That leaves God out of the equation, and James calls that evil boasting. Second, we do our homework. We pray. We study the Scriptures. We seek advice. We try to know God's heart on the matter. Then comes the tentative decision. "God, it *seems* as if this option fits within your will. If it's your will, let it happen. If it's not, shut it down."

Since we've prayed, "God, *if* this is your will, let it happen," we can rest. Then when it happens—and we believe God answers prayer—then we can validly assume it truly *is* within God's will for us. Think about the trust God has in us. When his Word doesn't guide us, God wants us to grow into making godly decisions that reflect his heart. Does God have plans for us? Absolutely. Does he encourage us to choose directions under his guidance? Absolutely. And that's the truth.

Log the Truth

1. Have you been told God has a specific plan for your life? If so, how has that affected your decisions and behavior?

2. Did you fully follow that plan of God's for you? Why or why not?

3. Have you experienced a time when you knew God did have a specific desire for your life? Describe it.

4. Have you experienced a time when God gave you great freedom to choose among several opportunities? What happened?

5. Has the "promise" of Jeremiah 29:11 brought discouragement to you? ("'For I know the plans I have for you,' declares the LORD, 'plans to prosper you and not to harm you, plans to give you hope and a future.'") Describe the situation.

6. Are you within God's will for your life regarding being saved? If not, what obstacles stand in your way? Are you ready to move past them?

7. Are you within God's will for your life regarding growing in Christ? If not, what obstacles stand in your way? Are you ready to move past them?

Lie 8

I'll Never Be a Billy Graham

The Truth about Our Ministry

Not long after I recommitted my life to Christ, I began to work with the youth group at the church I grew up in. I loved it! These young people exhibited a great openness to God coupled with a hunger to learn more. I became captivated by the privilege of spending time with them.

That experience led me to considering the professional youth ministry, which reopened a previously closed can of worms. I had gone to a Christian college five years before to prepare for a similar ministry, and it didn't work out at all. This time was different, though. Now ministry wasn't simply "doing the right thing" or an attempt to secure a sure ticket to heaven. Now I wanted the chance to expose others to the same joy I'd found in Christ.

Others encouraged me, but I resisted—strongly. I was ministering, and although I felt an urge to do more, I still fought it. Why? After a great deal of praying and pondering, I realized my hesitancy came mostly from a fear of failing. What if my current level of ministry was where I should stay? What if I wasn't talented or gifted enough to do it "professionally"? What if the youth group didn't grow, or what if we didn't reach new people or help them develop in Christ?

Those questions paralyzed me for some time. Since I couldn't know for sure, I just decided not to pursue youth ministry professionally. Then I realized that once more, I had believed a lie.

Identify the Lie

Too often, we Christians buy into the lie that we're not qualified for "significant" ministry, which may keep us from serving God as he would desire. In his recent book, *The State of the Church: 2002*, George Barna reveals interesting trends within churches. The year 1996 seems to be the low point of religious beliefs and behaviors for the last 15 years; only 37 percent of American adults attended church each week. However, by 2002, that number grew to an encouraging 43 percent.

No corresponding rise, however, came in numbers of those who volunteer at a church (ministry), those who pray, who attend a small group, or who participate in personal evangelism. What does that mean? More people go to church, but fewer serve at church.

I recently did an admittedly unscientific survey of some local congregations, hoping to clarify Barna's findings for myself. We've been told that 10 percent of church members do 90 percent of the work and that large churches have a smaller involvement ratio. I wanted to see if this commonly held belief had any truth behind it. I was surprised by my results.

Small churches—those under 200 in weekly adult worship attendance—had both the highest and lowest involvement ratios. Church A, with attendance averaging 150 adults, had just 20 percent involvement. Not surprisingly, their attendance has slipped over the last few years. Church B, with 120 adults in worship, achieved the highest at 65 percent. Again, not surprisingly, both their attendance and involvement ratios have increased lately.

Church C, averaging 1500 adults, involves 40 percent of them in ministry, while achieving significant growth. Church D has the fastest growth rate in the community, and 50 percent of their 1400 adults have a clear ministry.

What conclusions did I draw? When lay people get involved in ministry, good results. When Christians buy into the lie that ministry isn't for them, the church suffers. Let me suggest six dimensions of the lie that contribute to our lack of ministry involvement and influence how Christ's body carries out its God-given functions.

COMPARISONS SCARE US

When I first considered getting into the youth ministry, I talked to several successful youth pastors, and they convinced me, though unknowingly, I didn't measure up. When sharing my faith, I wasn't as effective as Billy Graham. When teaching, I wasn't as witty as Chuck Swindoll. When organizing a social outing, I wasn't as gregarious as Les Christie. Many of us size up the competition, decide we're not medal contenders, and avoid ministry altogether.

A LACK OF GIFTEDNESS DISABLES US

Many times we doubt our gifts and abilities. We look at the difficulty of the task and feel incompetent. We're afraid that we'll fail in ministry. Even the apostle Paul seems to have felt the same way about ministry, as revealed in 2 Corinthians 3:5: "Not that we are competent in ourselves …"

Perhaps I titled this section incorrectly. In truth, we perceive that we lack giftedness. That perception may not match reality, but our doubts are certainly real. We fear failing and refuse to make the attempt.

THE IMPORTANCE INTIMIDATES US

Ministry provides a marvelous opportunity to affect people's lives. When we do it well, people may accept Christ and go on to heaven. To lead others to Christ is an honor and a privilege like no other. If we inaccurately represent God, people may reject Christ and go to hell. My wife used to work at a doctor's office, and he regularly reminded the workers that a mistake could result in death (not their own!). They always had to use the utmost caution and judgment. Without minimizing physical consequences, if we make ministry mistakes, people may spend eternity in hell. That's a frightening thought!

Sometimes then, in fearing that result, we back off from ministry almost entirely. Better to leave such crucial tasks for someone who's better qualified, who knows the right answers. We may be bad news for people in their spiritual search!

THE CHALLENGE STRETCHES US

I learned a long time ago that the teacher learns far more than the student. When we take on ministry responsibilities, we get stretched. We have to grapple with the truths of the text and how they touch our lives before we can ever teach them to someone else. Attempting a difficult ministry requires that we rely more on God and his power than on ourselves.

So, what's the problem? We can't stay in our spiritual recliners, resting on the past. Ministry forces us to grow. Many of us almost subconsciously resist ministry because we realize we'll be forced to move deeper in our faith, beyond our comfort zone. Going into ministry compares to the theme song from the movie *Top Gun*, which says, "Heading to the danger zone, danger zone."

When we buy into the lie that we can avoid spiritual growth, ministry can be a threat to us.

THE OPTIONS DISTRACT US

For many of us, options may provide our most significant obstacle to ministry. We have so many choices of things to do, and personal evangelism and prayer meetings aren't very high on the list. Rather than teaching junior high boys, we want to go to the river twice a month. We enjoy getting blessed in the worship service, but we're not ready to commit to a small group. Or our time gets sucked up taking our children to sports and youth activities.

We tend to be consumers, not producers. We go to church for our benefit, not to share some of that benefit with others. And worst of all, we think that's okay.

Learn the Truth

God designed each Christian to be a minister, to be involved in serving. When we come to Christ, we don't just receive forgiveness. We receive a mission. A life purpose. A lifestyle. A ministry. Maybe paid, maybe not; maybe leading, maybe following; maybe college educated, or not. But we all minister.

Let's look at four principles that clarify this truth.

CONFIRM YOUR CALL

Back in high school, I mistakenly thought that ministry was for the professionals. Although we usually call them "pastors" now, we called them "ministers" back then. The rest of us were "members." We paid the freight; they did the work. We paid them to do the ministry, so we didn't have to. But that let us off the hook, didn't it?

In truth, God calls each follower of Jesus to be a minister. Some get paid; most do not. Some have college training to do their task; most do not. Some lead ministry teams; most do not. Some do just one ministry task, others do a variety over their years of serving. But all minister—in different ways, places, seasons, and styles as we see in this passage from Ephesians 4:

> It was he who gave some to be apostles, some to be prophets, some to be evangelists, and some to be pastors and teachers, to prepare *God's people for works of service*, so that the body of Christ may be built up until we all reach unity in the faith and in the knowledge of the Son of God and become mature, attaining to the whole measure of the fullness of Christ (vv. 11–13, emphasis added).

Leaders minister by motivating, training, and empowering God's people to do ministry. (The verse says "works of service," but we usually translate that as ministry.) Their goal is to help us grow in Christ so that we reach the fullness of Christ's character and heart.

What happens if the ministers (the people) don't confirm their call? The church doesn't grow in numbers or maturity, we don't have unity, and we don't achieve the fullness of Christ God desires for us. When we resist ministry, we resist God's design. We short-circuit what God wants the church to be.

Now, allow me to give some exceptions! When we're still searching for God or a local church, we may be best off to not get too involved in ministry. Commitment to a local church is a needed part of ministering with that body, and obvious problems result when we agree to volunteer and then don't even show up! Sometimes, though, even committed Christians need a season of rest and recovery. Dick and Sharon visited our church after I'd met them at a community event. They'd just gone through a painful church experience and needed time to heal. But our church was small, and we couldn't do all the tasks we wanted to do, which frustrated them. They wanted to be involved but needed healing.

We need to lovingly encourage those who need a season of recovery to take it, and then, when they are refreshed, to help them choose a ministry that best suits both the needs of the local body and those of the individual believers.

UNDERSTAND YOUR UNIQUENESS

Remember my fears that I couldn't evangelize like Billy Graham or teach like Chuck Swindoll? Turns out the fears were unfounded. God doesn't want me to teach or preach like anyone else. Nor does he want you to. He wants us to be the one-of-a-kind ministers *he* designed us to be. I have a **SHAPE** for ministry that Billy Graham absolutely cannot duplicate. I'm indebted to Rick Warren of Saddleback Valley Community Church for this acronym that puts together five qualities that make us all unique in our ministry. I heard this at the Purpose Driven Church seminar.

First, we have unique **S**piritual gifts, according to 1 Corinthians 12:7-10, 28-30.

> Now to each one the manifestation of the Spirit
> is given for the common good. To one there is

given through the Spirit the message of wisdom, to another the message of knowledge by means of the same Spirit, to another faith by the same Spirit, to another gifts of healing by that one Spirit, to another miraculous powers, to another prophecy, to another distinguishing between spirits, to another speaking in different kinds of tongues, and to still another the interpretation of tongues … And in the church God has appointed first of all apostles, second prophets, third teachers, then workers of miracles, also those having gifts of healing, those able to help others, those with gifts of administration, and those speaking in different kinds of tongues. Are all apostles? Are all prophets? Are all teachers? Do all work miracles? Do all have gifts of healing? Do all speak in tongues? Do all interpret?

God gifts each believer differently and then adds to our gifts our unique Heart—the thing that moves us, touches our emotions. Our heart forges our passions and gets our spiritual blood pumping. It's what leads us toward a particular arena of ministry.

Next, add our personal Abilities, the natural talents we were born with and the abilities we've developed over the years. Maybe we're gifted in teaching or encouraging or art or music. Then mix in our absolutely unique Personality. God made us introverted or extroverted, assertive or passive, to further craft a unique minister. God made us as we are, and he doesn't make mistakes. Our personalities will lead us into a ministry just right for us.

Last, blend in our Experiences, those that only we have. I would gladly wipe the miserable memories of junior high from my knowledge, but God has used those experiences to build in me compassion for people who don't quite fit in. As Rick Warren reminds us, "God never wastes a hurt." God often redeems our painful experiences by allowing us to develop a ministry to touch those experiencing what we went through.

So what do we have? The truth that God has created each of us with a unique **SHAPE** for ministry. We can't duplicate another's ministry. No one can duplicate ours. So again, if we don't minister, essential ministry goes undone.

RELEASE THE RESULTS

When I considered entering youth ministry, I feared failing, not being able to get the desired results. Then with great relief I found 1 Corinthians 3:6-7, which enabled me to let go of the responsibility for results. Paul says, "I planted the seed, Apollos watered it, but God made it grow. So neither he who plants nor he who waters is anything, but only God, who makes things grow."

What freedom! In our ministry, God expects us to do our task—planting, watering, teaching, leading, helping—to the best of our ability. Then we leave the results to him. That eliminates an invalid pride if results come, along with invalid discouragement if results don't come. We just focus on doing it and grab onto the truth that God doesn't hold us responsible for results.

RECEIVE YOUR REWARD

Here comes the good part! Even though we're not accountable for results, God still rewards us for our ministry efforts. Go down just a few verses from our last passage, keeping in mind the ministry context.

> The man who plants and the man who waters
> have one purpose, and each will be rewarded
> according to his own labor ... By the grace God
> has given me, I laid a foundation as an expert
> builder, and someone else is building on it. But
> each one should be careful how he builds. For
> no one can lay any foundation other than the
> one already laid, which is Jesus Christ. If any
> man builds on this foundation using gold, silver,
> costly stones, wood, hay or straw, his work will

be shown for what it is, because the Day will bring it to light. It will be revealed with fire, and the fire will test the quality of each man's work. If what he has built survives, he will receive his reward. If it is burned up, he will suffer loss; he himself will be saved, but only as one escaping through the flames (3:8, 10–15).

When we minister well, God will give us eternal rewards. When we minister poorly, or not at all, we'll enter heaven with the smell of smoke on our coattails. Yes, God calls us as ministers—every one of us. He's given us a unique ministry of serving and will reward us. And that's the truth!

Live the Truth

Let's explore four steps in developing our unique ministry.

GO WITH GOD

God's presence provides the foundation for ministry. We don't do it on our own power, with our gifts, abilities, and strengths. We do it with God. God called Joshua to lead his people after the death of Moses, and he gave three very specific principles that apply just as well to us today.

First, God gave Joshua a *ministry*: to lead the people into the Promised Land.

Second, God gave an *attitude* toward ministry: to be strong and courageous and not wimp out, draw back, or be afraid. Joshua was to consistently approach ministry with an overcomer's attitude.

Third, God *gave the means* to develop that attitude. Look at Joshua 1:9. "Have I not commanded you? Be strong and courageous. Do not be terrified; do not be discouraged, for the LORD your God *will be with you* wherever you go" (emphasis added).

I'm always encouraged by one of my favorite ministry lines: "If you want to see God act, then attempt something on his direction that is doomed to fail unless he is in it." Joshua took a rag-tag group of complaining former slaves and convinced them that their God went with them. Soon the hearts of their opponents melted in fear. Why? God went with them, and they were able to act with strength and courage (Joshua 2:11).

Our ministry fits the same pattern. Jesus gave the church a ministry task in Matthew 28:18–20. Notice the same empowerment.

> Then Jesus came to them and said, "All authority in heaven and on earth has been given to me. Therefore go and make disciples of all nations, baptizing them in the name of the Father and of the Son and of the Holy Spirit, and teaching them to obey everything I have commanded you. And surely *I am with you always*, to the very end of the age" (emphasis added).

Our ministry *task*: to reach the world with the joy of Jesus. Our ministry *means*: the presence of Jesus. I'm convinced that when we approach ministry with the attitude that we're privileged with the opportunity to work with God to accomplish his goals, then we can overcome our fears. That leads us to the next principle.

GO FOR IT

Yes, we fear all the pain and difficulties ministry can bring us. Get over it. Step out and do what God calls you to do. Experience what I call the "toad-kissing" phenomenon. You remember. Before you meet the handsome prince (or princess!) you have to kiss a lot of toads. (Please take that figuratively!)

Be adventurous and try different ministries. Frequently we won't find the ministry we love until we eliminate the ministries we don't enjoy. How else did I learn that teaching at a junior high school wasn't my life's calling? I did it for two years. I'm convinced now, though.

Realize that a ministry isn't a life sentence! You can always quit when God leads you in a different direction, despite what some pastors desire. Sometimes a ministry will be a perfect fit—for a while. Or maybe God wants you there as a piece of a larger puzzle. I sincerely believe God called me to one particular church, but after three years even a blockhead like me could realize this wasn't forever. But my stepdaughter met a young man in that town, and my wife and I now have two wonderful grandchildren. Then we ended up starting a new church in a growing town nearby, which was probably the most rewarding church ministry I've had.

Did God call me to the first church? Yes. Was that a permanent call? I don't believe so. Sometimes we finish what we can do in a particular spot, and we move on. I say all this to firmly drive home the principle: Try a lot of ministries, but don't expect each ministry to last forever. And even though a particular ministry may not last forever, being a minister does.

Go Together

We Americans tend to be an independent lot. We want to do it *our* way, and we value the strong self-reliant type. That may work well for hamburgers, but as we craft our ministry, we need to do so in conjunction with the church and other Christians. I'd like to suggest two basic reasons why: *synergy* and *support*.

Synergy basically says that $1 + 1 = 3$, or that the total is greater than the sum of the parts. When we work in concert, we do far more than we could on our own. In rock music, I probably most love hearing the thumping bass guitar as my chest vibrates with the sound. A dynamic drum solo always gets me going. And the virtuosity of a lead guitarist, fingers flying as he lays out the chords, fills me with awe.

But I like the band best of all. When you combine talented musicians, the result far exceeds what any individual does alone. That's how we work in the body of Christ as ministers: each with a unique role, but connected to accomplish tasks we couldn't dream of on our own. That teamwork shaped this book. I had the concept and went to the Mt. Hermon Christian Writers Conference, where a lot of people did a lot of work. There I met Mary McNeil, an editor at Cook Communications Ministries who caught the dream. She presented the idea to the publication committee at Cook, who decided to publish it. More editors improved the structure and wording. The finance crowd determined if it could affordably be published, how to price it, and how much could be spent on marketing. Marketing folks worked out how it could best be sold. Publicity people got the word out. The sales people went out to the bookstores and distributors, who sold it. You bought it (or borrowed it from a friend!). That's synergy. A lot of ministers working together on a ministry task that none of us could have done on our own.

Support means we're not alone. Others give ideas when we run dry, a shoulder to cry on, and cheerleading when we experience a victory. They also remind us that we're not Lone Rangers with everything depending on us. Sometimes you support me; sometimes I support you. We realize we're part of something bigger than ourselves.

Both concepts—synergy and support—come from 1 Corinthians 12.

> Now you are the body of Christ, and each one of
> you is a part of it. ... Now the body is not made
> up of one part but of many. If the foot should
> say, "Because I am not a hand, I do not belong to
> the body," it would not for that reason cease to
> be part of the body. ... Now to each one the
> manifestation of the Spirit is given for the
> common good ... (vv. 27, 14–15, 7).

Doing ministry together provides another way to fine tune what God designed you to do. Just as the human body recognizes the gifts of its various parts, so the body of Christ recognizes the giftedness of its members. I once thought God destined me for music. I loved it and wanted to play it. But every time I sang or played an instrument, I cleared the house. When I taught, however, people mentioned how blessed they were. See the difference?

You're a leader if you have followers. You're a teacher if you have students. Listen carefully to what others say. They may see gifts in you that you never even knew you had. That's happened to me on occasion. I just ministered, and tasks got done without my even knowing I was using one of my gifts. That's why we need to go into ministry together.

GO IN SUCCESS

Few of us would see a point to pouring time and energy into anything that didn't yield results. We all want to succeed, so how can we guarantee success in our ministry? By doing the only task that is within our grasp: being faithful to do the task God's called us to do. We're to plant or water or teach or encourage or give or help to the best of our ability. God alone is responsible for the results as we saw in 1 Corinthians 3:6–7.

When success comes, it's easy to take personal credit and get a big head. When success doesn't come, though, it's easy to take that personally as well, and get discouraged. Successful ministry means we do our job. To the best of our ability. Then we leave the rest to God.

I encourage you to not allow discouragement to keep you from ministering. God has uniquely gifted and crafted you for a special job in his kingdom. And that's the truth.

Log the Truth

1. Do you feel competent to do significant ministry? Why or why not?

2. Has the importance of ministry inhibited you? How?

3. What are the major reasons you may have resisted getting more involved in ministry?

4. Do you truly understand that you have a unique ministry no one else can do? How does this affect your attitude toward ministry?

5. How does knowing that you aren't responsible for the results change how you view ministry? ("I planted the seed, Apollos watered it, but God made it grow. So neither he who plants nor he who waters is anything, but only God, who makes things grow" [1 Corinthians 3:6-7].)

6. How does the concept of working together in ministry change your view of its challenges and rewards?

Lie 9

Christianity Is Great on Sundays

The Truth about Passion

Melissa grew up in a small church in the Northwest and enjoyed expressing her love of music by playing the piano during worship. But during those teen years, her questioning mind struggled with the difference between what so many members said on Sunday and what they did the rest of the week. Their hypocrisy, her rebellious streak, and the freedom of the '60s combined to lead her out of church, although she took with her a residual belief in some sort of God.

She blended yoga and astrology and strove to be a good, moral person. She thought she succeeded, but in her mid 40s, uncertainty led her to circle back. Her family began praying at meals. They looked for a local church. She grew more open to God. Then, while Melissa was still searching, someone ran a red light. Her journey ended.

I performed her memorial service and grieved. Had she followed that returning circle far enough? I didn't know, although the family wanted to believe so. We all grieved over the wasted years she spent away from God.

Yes, Melissa bore responsibility for how she chose to react to the church members' hypocrisy, but they also carried some guilt. If you're not sure of that, take a quick break and read

Ezekiel 33:1-12 and Matthew 18:5-7. Our behavior influences others, and God holds us accountable.

Those church members bought into the lie that Christianity was good on Sundays but shouldn't affect the rest of the week. They didn't get too carried away by their faith. And Melissa paid part of the price for their acceptance of untruth.

Identify the Lie

Statistics abound that affirm Melissa's church experience. Studies repeatedly reveal that sinful behaviors such as marital unfaithfulness, teen pregnancy, and divorce occur just as frequently among those claiming faith as those who do not. Eighty percent of Americans say that God is very important to them, but half of those demonstrate that God isn't important enough to worship regularly in a local congregation.

The year 2002 assailed us with now-familiar failures in corporate ethics. Flawed accounting, misstated profits and/or losses, and stock manipulations abounded. Often, Christians led the list of offenders. As told in *Christianity Today* on August 13, 2002, *Fortune* magazine listed its twenty-five greediest executives. Heading the list: Philip Anschutz of Qwest, well known in sports and entertainment. Yet, he bankrolled the Narnia films to do "something significant in American Christianity." Steve Case of AOL Time Warner came in at the third spot. You may have heard of Case's $8.3 million donation to Dr. James Kennedy's ministry. The Rigas family created Adelphia, one of the largest cable providers in the country. They looted the firm of millions, drove it into bankruptcy, now face legal charges, and still proclaim their faith. Ken Lay of Enron may lead the list of those tarred with the brush of being ethically challenged. Yet in a May 18, 2001, interview with *The Door* magazine, he both proclaimed his life-long faith in Christ and his certainty that God called him to business "to make a bigger and more positive impact … than … the ministry." We can't doubt the size of his impact, only who it benefited.

The problem here is not that Christian businesspeople failed and didn't avoid sin. The problem is the glaring inconsistency of their Christian profession with their new ethical reputation. Somehow their faith didn't translate into how they did business. By their behavior, they loudly proclaimed the lie: Church is great on Sundays, but it shouldn't interfere with business practices Monday through Friday.

We want God in measured doses—just enough God to make us feel good, but not enough to make us fanatics. Wilbur Reese expresses this idea well in something I found on the Internet.

> I would like to buy $3.00 worth of God, please.
> Not enough to explode my soul or disturb my
> sleep, but just enough to buy a cup of warm
> milk or a snooze in the sunshine. I don't want
> enough to love a black man or pick beets with a
> migrant. I want ecstasy, not transformation. I
> want the warmth of the womb, not a new birth.
> I want a pound of the Eternal in a paper sack. I
> would like to buy $3.00 worth of God, please.

We want to control God, not be consumed by him. And what do we call those who take their walk with God seriously and commit their lives to him? Lou Carroll, in a short piece in *Lookout* magazine, has the answer.

> I'm a Christian and I'm a football fan. I get
> excited about football. I've been known to yell
> and shout ... I get excited about the draft,
> training camp, and the new schedule ... I
> suppose I get a little crazy over it all. However,
> my friends don't think it's unusual ... no one
> thinks I'm weird, crazy, or strange. When I get
> excited about football, my behavior is considered normal.
>
> I get excited about the Lord, too. When I spend
> a lot of time talking about Christ and salvation,
> my friends become uncomfortable. They give
> me strange looks and knowing smiles ... [they]
> consider this behavior a bit excessive. Their

expressions say, "religious fanatic." Occasionally their words say, "You better take it easy on that stuff."

Why am I a fan when I get excited about football, but a fanatic when I get excited about God?

Many define a religious fanatic as someone two levels above them on the commitment ladder, someone crazy enough to let their beliefs about God change their behavior. Someone described the range of commitment to God, "In all Christians, Christ is present; in some Christians, Christ is prominent; in a few Christians, Christ is preeminent." The "few" many call fanatics.

Of course, there is a negative form of fanaticism. Jim Fowler, a pastor friend, describes fanatics as "forgetting their purpose, they double their speed." The novelist Morris West warns, "Beware the blind passion of the moth seeking the flame." Action and zeal don't prove the rightness of the cause. True religious fanatics, in the most negative sense, have no foundation of biblical truth or common sense.

Many believe faith should be private, kept out of politics, business ethics, and other realms of our lives. We don't mix faith and behavior any more than we mix church and state. Why? Because it's more comfortable to place Christianity on our list of priorities, but not at the top; it's more comfortable to allow other values to take precedence over God's values; and it's more comfortable to justify ethical shortcuts by saying we *need* to just to make a living.

Just what *is* true? How do we balance being imperfect people with living as God's people? Let's explore these questions.

Learn the Truth

If we fall prey to the lie that we can limit our Christianity to Sundays, then we come into the truth when we realize that true faith places God at the highest priority in our lives. We often call that *passion*. By passion I don't mean we get weird or strange, nor do I mean we get on an emotional peak. Passion speaks of *priorities* and *progress*.

Priorities: What do we most value? Progress: Where are we going? When we combine the two we come to a convicting question: Are we willing to change the direction of our lives to match our values?

PRIORITIES

When God is our priority, we love him more than anything else. We value him above all. We acknowledge Jesus as the CEO of our lives. With apologies to fans of Bruce Springsteen, Jesus *is* The Boss. In Matthew 22:35-36, an expert in the Law of Moses asks him to identify the most important commandment. In verses 37-38, Jesus describes the priority of passion: "'Love the Lord your God with all your heart and with all your soul and with all your mind.' This is the first and greatest commandment."

Jesus didn't come up with a new concept in his conversation with the man. Back in Deuteronomy 6:5, packed into a book filled with details of what the people of God should do, God told them, "Love the LORD your God with all your heart and with all your soul and with all your strength."

I found nineteen other times in Deuteronomy when God gave the same basic principle: Love God above all else. It sounds great, but I must admit I struggled with this concept—for years!

During my college years of searching, two friends and I grabbed the chance for a week of Sierra fishing to renew our friendship, philosophize as college students do, and catch a few trout. We each attended Christian colleges, but I now had my doubts about what being a Christian really meant. Those doubts didn't plague them, and I hoped they could help me in my quest.

As Gabe's aging VW beetle chugged through the night, I popped the question: "Guys, how committed does a Christian have to be? I mean, do you have to be on fire? Or is it okay to just be one, but not get too fanatical?"

That topic ate up a hundred miles or more. Their consensus favored the latter, but I couldn't quite rest at that and began a quest for essential Christianity that lasted several years. Just what does it mean to be a Christian? What are the standards? How closely do we have to live up to them? Must we live up to them at all? Can we find a balance between those Christians who profess some vague "belief" in Jesus, in which case faith means almost nothing, and those who require pure commitment, in which case faith becomes almost impossible?

This section summarizes what I learned on my journey to find the essential Christian life. No being overly harsh. No wimping out either. No lies.

The Bible uses the word "passion" numerous times, usually referring to emotions or the strong temptation to sin. Only once do we find passion used in a clearly positive manner. The King James Version refers to Jesus' death and burial as his "passion." Not temptation, not emotion, but his willingness to endure difficulty and pain to achieve a goal.

We have passion for God when knowing him holds more value than anything else and we're willing to change our lives to reach that goal and to serve him. Simple to understand, isn't it? That's loving God with all our heart, soul, mind, and strength. Passion doesn't fit God into our empty spaces; passion fits our lives into God's place.

Passion doesn't praise God on Sunday and live as we please on Saturday night. Passion isn't teaching a Sunday school class and underreporting our income at tax time. Now, passion isn't perfection, but the heart of the Christian life is making God our top priority.

Progress

While passion for God may result from a decision we make at one point in time, we progress into living out that priority. We craft our lives to both express and reach that passion. We obey. James the brother of Christ asked the question of how essential obedience is for a genuine love of God: "What good is it, my brothers, if a man claims to have faith but has no deeds? Can such faith save him?" (James 2:14).

James 2:20–24 provides the answer.

> You foolish man, do you want evidence that faith without deeds is useless? Was not our ancestor Abraham considered righteous for

what he did when he offered his son Isaac on the altar? You see that his faith and his actions were working together, and his faith was made complete by what he did. And the scripture was fulfilled that says, "Abraham believed God, and it was credited to him as righteousness," and he was called God's friend. You see that a person is justified by what he does and not by faith alone.

I've noticed a fascinating dual connection on this issue of belief and behavior. James said we can't believe and not behave. On the one hand, our behavior demonstrates our belief, our conviction that we love God above all. It provides evidence of the inward reality. (What do we call a person who claims faith but doesn't have a life change? A hypocrite—the type of Christian that drove Melissa away from church.) A changing life demonstrates a genuine love of God.

On the other hand, our behavior also increases our belief. I can directly trace my closeness with God to the time I spend reading the Bible, praying, serving him, and loving others. The more I do those acts, the more intimate I get with him.

Funny, isn't it? We start with believing, and then we act to express that belief. Our actions cause our belief to strengthen. What does that increased faith cause? More obedience, which leads to ... well, you get the picture! We live as Jesus would have us live, and our lives get closer to Jesus. Not a bad deal.

If we want passion in our lives, we need to act like we have it. Obey God's commands. Spend time alone with God. Serve others. Your passion will grow—not instantly, not all at once. When you look at the overall direction, though, you'll see the change. You'll see progress.

You may think this sounds almost impossible: to love God with *all* our heart, soul, mind, and strength. None of us do that perfectly, so are we not Christians then? This brings us to that quandary I struggled with on the Sierra trip. How can we balance the "Christian" life that has no behavior change with the apparently impossible call to love God with all our being? How can we follow Jesus' impossible command in John 14:15: "If you love me, you *will obey* what I command"?

GROW INTO IT

Perhaps the most stupid act I've ever done on a motorcycle was attempting to drive 900 miles across the state of Texas in one day—on just two hours of sleep. But at twenty-six I thought I could do anything. I learned I couldn't. But I also learned I could make it forty miles to a rest area, get a cup of coffee and a doughnut, and drive forty miles more. I repeated the process for hundreds of miles, and as you can tell, I survived. My experience provides a pattern for the spiritual life

When I first made God the ultimate priority in my life, I asked him to change a specific area that I knew wasn't right. With his help I could do that one thing, we made some progress, and I was ready to rest. I'd arrived! God gently pointed out another area, we worked on that; then came the next rest stop with just enough time for coffee and a doughnut, so to speak.

God continues to reveal dimensions in my life that need repair or rebuilding. So far, I've hit a lot of rest stops, but I haven't yet reached the destination of loving God with all my being. It's called progress.

During growth spurts in my early teens, I often got an article of clothing much too big along with the comment, "Well, you'll *grow into it.*" I hated wearing a tent in hopes that for two weeks, a year later, the clothes would fit before I grew out of them. God knows that once we establish a goal of loving him above all, and regularly and ruthlessly give up whatever doesn't help us, we'll grow into acting on our decision. Not that we're perfect, but we truly desire to move toward him.

God gives us salvation; we just need to grow into it. Paul understood that, as we see in 2 Corinthians 3:18, "And we, who with unveiled faces all reflect the Lord's glory, are being transformed into his likeness with *ever-increasing glory*, which comes from the Lord, who is the Spirit" (emphasis added).

The Revised Standard Version says, "from one stage of glory to another." God expects progression, not perfection.

Loving and obeying God then means we give all we know of ourselves to all we know of God, and keep adjusting the formula as we learn. Realize that we each combine belief and unbelief, obedience and failure. The side we pay the most attention to wins. Let's not beat ourselves up for a lack of perfection. But when we don't place God at the top priority, the feeling we get is guilt—valid guilt.

In Revelation 3:15-16, Jesus spoke to church members and described his expectation for passion in the Christian life: "I know your deeds, that you are neither cold nor hot. I wish you were either one or the other! So, because you are lukewarm—neither hot nor cold—I am about to spit you out of my mouth." God wants passion in our lives—not perfection, but passion. A fire for him. Valuing him above all. Now, how do we get there?

Live the Truth

How can we balance the tension between the passion we know we should have and our failure to achieve it? Let me suggest two steps, and as we examine them, let's commit to stark honesty in evaluating just where we stand.

WANT IT

We begin to build passion when we decide we truly want it. Passion can be an all-consuming fire that, once kindled, runs its course. God doesn't want us to make hasty decisions without considering the implications.

I once studied all of Jesus' "evangelism accounts" to learn his style. He surprised me with his no-holds-barred, take-no-prisoners attitude. An extended passage in Luke 14 gives one example. Let's look first at his warning to decision-makers in verses 28–32.

> Suppose one of you wants to build a tower. Will
> he not first sit down and estimate the cost to see
> if he has enough money to complete it? For if he
> lays the foundation and is not able to finish it,
> everyone who sees it will ridicule him, saying,
> "This fellow began to build and was not able to

finish." Or suppose a king is about to go to war against another king. Will he not first sit down and consider whether he is able with ten thousand men to oppose the one coming against him with twenty thousand? If he is not able, he will send a delegation while the other is still a long way off and will ask for terms of peace.

Before people decide, Jesus tells them to carefully count the cost. See what the decision entails. Know what you're committing yourself to.

Now, what cost does Jesus refer to? Giving everything we have. Examine verses 26–27 and 33.

If anyone comes to me and does not *hate* his father and mother, his wife and children, his brothers and sisters—yes, even his own life—he cannot be my disciple. And anyone who does not *carry his cross* and follow me cannot be my disciple. … In the same way, any of you who *does not give up everything he has* cannot be my disciple (emphasis added).

Notice the cost. We must love God so much that our love for family and self seems like hatred. We must carry our cross, not placing limits on how far we'll follow God. We must give up everything to the Lordship of Christ. Or what? Or we *cannot* be his disciples. Direct words from Jesus.

Know the cost—all we have. Count it first—know what you're committing to before making your decision. Given the high cost, why should we want it?

First, *it's true.* Jesus doesn't practice "bait and switch," where he entices us with a low level of commitment only to increase it once we're in. Jesus clearly states the degree of our wanting him that's necessary. Remember, we're talking about desire, not perfect action here! We need to continually keep that in mind. Jesus consistently gave the same message. I've never found a single example of Jesus encouraging or allowing anything less than passionately loving God as number one in our lives. That means the lukewarm Christian life has no assurance of being the Christian life at all.

Second, *God is worth it.* Nothing matches the value we find in God when we give our all to him. You might want to begin a study of the benefits of knowing God as Jesus described it. Jot down all the good things that come to mind. Then count the cost. Examine the downside, the disadvantages of passion. Have no doubt; they exist. Check out both sides before deciding.

Once we've looked at both the advantages and disadvantages of loving God, we make our decision. Assured that there is no better way to live, we make a conscious commitment to love God with all our heart, soul, mind, and strength. We acknowledge we fail in some areas, but our first priority is to know him. This decision becomes a landmark of our lives. When doubts arise later, as they surely will, we go back to our decision.

After my years of questions and searching, in February 1971, I knelt by my bed and prayed, "God, I can't make my life what it should be. I think you can. You have complete permission to make any changes you desire."

He did, he is, and he will. And in the difficult times, I go back to that point in time when I decided I wanted to build a passion for God. It was a step in the right direction, but living a life of passion takes more than a prayer.

ACT ON IT

Once we decide to love God the most, then we act. We choose behavior that expresses the character of God, and reject that which doesn't. Trust me, this becomes a lifelong process. On the morning I began writing this section, for my devotions I read Colossians 1:15-20, which expresses the absolute supremacy of Christ—pretty much what we've been working on in this chapter.

I prayed through it, asking God to help me live out the truth of Jesus' preeminence. Twenty minutes later, I began to do something—not a clear sin, not even close to what we'd typically call wrong. But, honestly, an almost audible voice asked, "Does this represent my supremacy in your life?"

I knew it didn't, so I started to ignore the voice, which began to fade a bit. Was I quenching God's Spirit in order to do something that I wanted but God didn't? That cost became higher than I was willing to pay. My choosing to listen to the Holy Spirit and turning away from what I was doing caused me to move closer to living out a desire for passion. Coincidence? I don't think so. It was just another step in the journey I began thirty-one years ago: trying to live in a way that shows I value God above all.

And that's the truth.

Log the Truth

1. Have you bought into the lie that Christianity should be left to Sundays? How has that belief affected your life day to day?

2. Why do you think it's easier to prefer God in measured doses?

3. What makes it so difficult to live out God's command to love him with all of our being?

4. Have you noticed how your behavior increases the depth of your beliefs? Describe how that works for you.

5. Are you seeing progress in your pursuit of growing more passionate about God? If not, what steps can you take to move forward?

6. Are you willing to pay the price for developing passion? Why or why not?

Lie 10

I'm Like This Because Mom Was a Nag

The Truth about Personal Responsibility

T he summer of 2001 captivated us with a political and spiritual lesson. A rising political career self-destructed, mostly due to a lack of candor and an unwillingness to take responsibility. Washington, D.C., intern Chandra Levy disappeared in late spring, and attention quickly turned to married California Congressman Gary Condit. (Let me make absolutely clear that no evidence was known then or at the time of this writing that incriminated Condit in Levy's death.)

Rumors of a Condit-Levy affair arose, which Condit quickly denied. When evidence for the affair grew and rumors of other affairs surfaced, Condit finally granted an interview. He merely acknowledged that he was "not perfect" and then proceeded to blame everyone but himself. The media, political opponents, and even the mother of Levy all came in for their share of responsibility. When the remains of Chandra were found, his attorney blasted the Washington, D.C., police.

Only the tragedy of September 11 pulled our attention away. Just a few months later, Condit lost the Democratic primary in "Condit country," his previously impregnable stronghold. Why? Certainly, politicians can survive affairs. We've seen that often enough. And no evidence linked Condit to the disappearance and death of Levy.

The public, however, was outraged at Condit's lack of responsibility. Perhaps he bought into the lie that we are who we are because of what others do. We're victims, helpless pawns, merely reacting to the actions of others.

Identify the Lie

People commonly shift the responsibility for what they do onto others. "I'm critical of others because Mom always nagged me." "I try to please people because I never received approval from my father." "I don't go to church because I've seen too many hypocrites there." We've all heard those excuses, haven't we? Often, we've used them ourselves.

Not long ago my wife and I drove over to the next town to pick up our grandkids for a few days. We saw a bumper sticker that simply said, "I didn't do it," and we laughed about getting one for each of the grandkids. Just after we arrived at their home, our son-in-law, David, got on Josh for something, and Josh quickly replied, "I didn't do it!" We roared, and David and Teri thought we'd gone crazy—until we explained the sign, and we all laughed together.

First Church battled every pastor it had, except for the founding one. Any expression of pastoral leadership became a target of suspicion and mistrust. Their rationale? The many affairs of their founding pastor made them mistrust pastors in general.

"You drove me into her arms," was Aaron's excuse. His wife Julie truly had neglected his emotional needs. Caught up in her own career, she had little time for him. So when one of his coworkers regularly expressed her appreciation, his resistance melted. Julie then blamed him for the breakup of their marriage, and he blamed her. Could both have been right?

Recent FBI statistics reveal that 30 percent of child abusers were themselves sexually abused as children. That means 70 percent of abused children overcome their backgrounds and do not become abusers. Does childhood sexual abuse impact our behavior? Apparently. But does it determine our future? Apparently not.

All of these stories share a common thread: We tend to blame others for what we do. Underlying this we find the concept of *stimulus and response*. A tourist watched a black-smith working on a hot horseshoe at colonial Williamsburg. The blacksmith tossed the shoe into a corner, and the tourist asked if he could touch it. The blacksmith grinned his assent; the tourist picked up and promptly dropped the still hot shoe.

"Kind of hot, isn't it?" said the smith.

The tourist replied, "No, it's not hot. Just doesn't take me long to hold a horseshoe!"

The stimulus: being burnt. The response: dropping the shoe. The stimulus led to the response, or the burning caused the dropping. You teach a dog a trick by rewarding certain behavior. Not being entirely stupid, the dog repeats the behavior to gain the reward. We cause certain behavior by providing the proper stimulus.

Our question: Does a certain stimulus *cause* the behavior? If we can answer yes, then we can avoid responsibility for what we do. Something *caused* us to act like that. We're not at fault; others made us do it. And that's a lie.

Learn the Truth

Two biblical principles have helped me understand this whole area of individual responsibility. As we find in so many areas, a tension exists between two true and seemingly contradictory concepts. First, our behavior certainly impacts others. We definitely *influence* them. Second, we don't *make* them react. They choose their responses.

UNDERSTAND INFLUENCE

John Donne expressed our interconnectedness with his classic line, "No man is an island." In an increasingly global world, the acts of one person affect others more and more.

My entire life has been influenced by others. I grew to love God by watching my mom live out her faith. I grew to value integrity by watching my dad make moral decisions. The gentle but firm encouragement of an optometrist in Taos, New Mexico, led me back to the ministry. The senior pastor's decision to hire me as an associate pastor at the Lawndale Christian Church changed the course of my life. Not only did I meet my wife there, but the job led to my becoming the senior pastor at a church in Fallbrook. In that town my stepdaughter met a man, married him, and presented us with our two much-loved grandchildren.

Each person who has touched my life has played some role in shaping who I am today. I'm sure the same is true for you. We cannot avoid being influenced by and influencing others.

In the first century, nearly all the meat sold in markets had been sacrificed to idols. The early Christians struggled over the issue. Should they eat that meat? Some said since idols were just statues, there wasn't even a problem. Others said they should avoid any appearance of doing what is wrong. They thought eating the meat was acknowledging the divinity of the idols. Paul resolved the quandary in Romans 14:19–21, where he discussed the principle of understanding influence.

> Let us therefore make every effort to do what leads to peace and to mutual edification. Do not destroy the work of God for the sake of food. All food is clean, but it is wrong for a man to eat anything that *causes* someone else to stumble. It is better not to eat meat or drink wine or to do anything else that will *cause* your brother to fall (emphasis added).

Was eating such meat inherently wrong? No. Was it wrong for some individuals? Yes. Paul asserted that we should avoid behavior that influences another person to do something that violates his or her conscience.

Here's another case. Pretend your friend Michael has a drinking problem and can't stop with just one beer. You know this, but you don't have the problem and see nothing wrong with having a beer or two. You and Michael go to a football ball game; you go for refreshments and bring back two beers, one for each of you. Michael drinks that beer—and five more until he's sloshed. Is Michael responsible for accepting that first beer and continuing to drink? Absolutely, but you also bear some responsibility for influencing him to do something that for him is wrong.

Influence can also work positively. Look back at the examples I mentioned in the beginning of this section. The biblical concepts of leadership, teaching, and mutual ministry all flow from the fact that we influence others. Influence allows us the privilege of helping others come to Christ, to grow, to become reproducing followers. Every Christian book is written to influence the readers toward growth. Every sermon is given to influence the hearers toward a deeper walk with Jesus.

UNDERSTAND PERSONAL RESPONSIBILITY

Influence, however, is limited in its, well, influence. It doesn't make us do things. Clearly, God gifts us with choice, with individual responsibility. Perhaps the most common passage establishing choice is Joshua 24:14–15:

> Now fear the LORD and serve him with all faithfulness. Throw away the gods your forefathers worshiped beyond the River and in Egypt, and serve the LORD. But if serving the LORD seems undesirable to you, then *choose for yourselves* this day whom you will serve, whether the gods your forefathers served beyond the River, or the gods of the Amorites, in whose land you are living. But as for me and my household, we will serve the LORD (emphasis added).

Joshua presented the people with a choice: God or other gods. Just choose. We can choose what we do. That means we can also choose how we respond to the stimuli of our lives.

Let's avoid determinism, the belief that gives birth to the lie we've discussed. It says we have little choice in our responses. For example, if I get angry and say to my wife, "You make me mad," am I telling the truth? Determinism states that a certain stimulus will bring a specific response.

Dr. Dave Jensen of Rockhurst University disagrees and describes the most profound truth he's ever learned: "Between stimulus and response is a place called choice." Remember the

FBI report that 30 percent of those sexually abused as children become abusers? That's influence. But 70 percent *do not* become abusers. That's choice.

If we *choose our response*, then we become *responsible*. Makes sense, doesn't it? David Reynolds discovered a worker who understood that well. A newcomer to Washington, he hired a local guy to take down a fir tree that threatened to fall on his house. They agreed on a modest price, and Reynolds asked about his liability insurance. He had none and went on to explain why. "If you want that kind of insurance, call Seattle. I'm willing to leave my truck right where it is." The location? Halfway between the tree and the house. That's responsibility.

Contrast that with the victim mentality we continually see. Charles Colson in his Breakpoint Commentary of August 22, 2002, told of an FBI agent who was fired for embezzling $2,000, which he used for gambling. The agent then sued the Bureau, arguing that his gambling behavior constituted a handicap, which was protected under the Americans with Disabilities Act. The court ordered the FBI to reinstate him.

Even when the courts don't, God holds us accountable for our decisions. Yes, others influence us, but we're not to be passive victims who take no responsibility.

I recently discovered a fascinating passage that deals with God's view of responsibility. Here's the story from Ezekiel 18. Apparently some people were misusing the saying, "The fathers eat sour grapes, and the children's teeth are set on edge" (v. 2). They encouraged a victim mentality.

God responded, as he always does, with truth: "The soul who sins is the one who will die" (v. 4). That's individual responsibility. God then talked about a certain righteous man who would live. That man, however, had an unrighteous son who faced spiritual death for his sins, despite the righteousness of his father. The grandson saw the evil acts of his father and didn't do the same things. Although his father was evil, the son was righteous and received life. God evaluated each man on the basis of what he had done individually.

God concludes in verse 30, "Therefore, O house of Israel, I will judge you, *each one according to his ways*" (emphasis added).

The acts of others influence us. We then choose how we respond. God holds us responsible for those choices. See the tension between influence and responsibility? God clarifies that later in Ezekiel 33:7–9:

> Son of man, I have made you a watchman for the house of Israel; so hear the word I speak and give them warning from me. When I say to the wicked, "O wicked man, you will surely die," and you do not speak out to dissuade him from his ways, that wicked man will die for his sin, and I will hold you accountable for his blood. But if you do warn the wicked man to turn from his ways and he does not do so, he will die for his sin, but you will have saved yourself.

God holds us accountable for how we influence others. God also holds us accountable for our responses to their influences on us. How do we live with all this tension and responsibility?

Live the Truth

These five steps will help us strike a practical balance between the sometimes-contradictory truths of influence and responsibility.

1. MAKE OUR CHOICES

When I was about nine or ten, I started spending a week or so each summer with an aunt and uncle who then had no children of their own. I thought it was a great adventure and felt sorry for my parents who didn't have my company for that time. (Only later did I realize this was their vacation each summer!)

What I probably loved the most about the week was getting to do what I never got to do at home—choose what we'd have for dinner. Mom was a great cook and had a number of dishes she fixed regularly. We understood, though, that she was the menu planner; ours definitely wasn't a short-order house. I remember the first afternoon I stayed with Dorothy and Bud, and Aunt Dorothy asked me what I'd like for dinner. No one had ever asked me that before! The decision was totally beyond me; I was stumped. Since I loved most kinds of food, and still do, I said I didn't care. Dorothy didn't let it rest. "But if you had your druthers, what would you druther eat?" That put dinner in a new perspective! One that I instantly liked, although I knew Mom would never go for it. But here, I could choose dinner. Obviously, my choices were limited by what was in the house on a given day, which made for some strange combinations at times, but we all laughed and enjoyed it.

Isn't that a step in growing up? Learning to make decisions for ourselves—making some bad ones and learning from them, and making some good ones and learning from those as well, enjoying our ability to shape our lives.

What a metaphor for our lives! God wants us to choose. He wants us to learn how to make decisions in a grown-up and godly manner, according to Hebrews 5:14, "But solid food is for the mature, who by constant use have trained themselves to distinguish good from evil."

We become spiritually mature as we continually make choices and learn to identify wise from foolish ones. So, don't fear making choices. God wants you to, according to Proverbs 16:9: "In his heart a man plans his course, but the Lord determines his steps." He won't leave us alone in the process, but he wants us to make plans, decide, and learn how to do that well. Now comes the good news.

2. Use God's Spiritual Power

Wanda Painter may be one of the greatest bakers in the western United States; and best of all, she attended our small group! She'd regularly bring some marvelous dessert she'd dreamed up, and once one of the other members commented that the concoctions might even be sinful since they tasted so good! He revealed his mistaken belief that anything so pleasurable had to be wrong!

In a stroke of theological genius, I replied no. My reasoning? All temptations can be resisted, according to 1 Corinthians 10:13. Since Wanda's creations were irresistible, they certainly couldn't be sinful. Makes sort of a twisted sense, doesn't it?

God provides all the power we need to resist temptation and follow him. Read Philippians 4:13, and watch all your excuses disappear as quickly as Wanda's goodies: "I can do everything through him who gives me strength."

Obviously, God doesn't promise me I can succeed in professional football at age fifty-four, even though I played in our church's flag league this spring. (I did pretty well, catching half a dozen passes in our first game. My career was cut short, though, when I tore my Achilles tendon in the second game.) Any situation with spiritual implications can be dealt with victoriously if we choose to appropriate the power God makes available to us.

When we face spiritual situations, we're not helpless victims. We're not powerless. Granted, our past may be difficult to overcome, and others often make decisions that negatively affect our lives. But we can repeat Philippians 4:13 as a reminder that we can choose wisely in God's strength and power then move forward. That leads us to our next step.

3. OWN OUR DECISIONS

When I was in my early twenties and teaching junior high, I took my science students to the medical school at the University of Southern California and was entranced by the idea of pursuing a medical career. I pondered going to med school and becoming a medical missionary. But when I learned about the difficulty of the courses, the time required, and the high tuition, I decided not to follow through on it.

I could have blamed my choice on the high costs of education. I could have blamed my schedule or my family for why I'm not a doctor today. The truth is, I didn't value being a doctor enough to pay the price. I wasn't a victim; I made a choice that I'm fully willing to accept and live with.

If God wants us to choose and if he provides the resources to live successfully in the spiritual realm, then we're responsible for our decisions. We own them. We choose our paths, and God directs our steps. Blaming others only stalls our progress. "You make me mad" should be banished from our vocabulary, along with "I'd be a better husband if you'd be a better wife." In fact, we could eliminate most sentences that start "If only you would . . ." and end with "then I would . . . ." Shifting responsibility simply doesn't relieve us of the consequences—good or bad—of our decisions.

At Aunt Dorothy's house, we choked down more than a few less-than-appetizing meals, but what happens when our decisions affect lives in a more serious way?

4. Admit Our Mistakes

As I shared in a previous chapter, I battled low self-esteem for years. Admitting wrongs just decreased the little esteem I had, so I didn't own up to much. That behavior brought great damage to a number of relationships, including my marriage.

As I've learned to understand the innate value God places on me, I'm learning that admitting mistakes brings great freedom. Rather than blaming others, rather than denying what's real, I discover relief in simply saying, "I was wrong. I made a bad decision."

Not long ago, I shared some personal struggles and sins with a group of men from our church. When I mentioned that to my wife, she responded with a huge hug and said, "I'm so proud of you for doing that." She well knew how hard it's been for me to admit a wrong.

I've learned that whether I make good decisions or bad, God loves me anyway. Just as much as he did before. And true friends do the same. (The wrongness of my decision usually isn't a surprise to them!) Admitting our bad decisions then leads to the next step.

5. MAKE IT RIGHT

About two years ago, we got a great price on a used Mustang convertible. We knew it wouldn't be long before we had to replace the engine, so the seller adjusted the price to compensate. Not long after we had it replaced, the "check engine" light came on—sporadically. Our mechanic got a probable read on the cause, a failing fuel pump. Unfortunately, the gas tank had to be removed to reach the pump. Not cheap, but no "check engine" light!

Until two days ago. Even with the computer codes, we can't figure out the problem. Until we do, the problem can't be fixed. Only when we identify a problem or mistakes we can make it right.

We first make our mistakes right by *changing our behavior*. Whatever we did wrong, we stop doing. Whatever we didn't do that we should have, we start doing. I struggled with a particular temptation for decades and would never admit it—or that it was really that bad—until it exploded on me. My closeness with God was shaken, significant relationships experienced damage. I finally acknowledged how wrong and severe that behavior was, which allowed God to make some major changes in me. But he couldn't do that until I acknowledged that I had made some wrong behavioral decisions.

We can't get our lives back on track until we admit we got off track. God wants to continue his work in us. We all need the message of Philippians 1:6: "being confident of this, that he who began a good work in you will carry it on to completion until the day of Christ Jesus."

Second, we make our mistakes right by *restoring others*. Remember influence? If our acts have brought a negative influence to others, we need to deal with that. Minimally, we need to give back what we've taken from them by admitting our wrong and asking forgiveness. When we admit that we wronged them, we begin the process of healing.

We're responsible for who we are and what we do, for our influence and for our response to the influence of others. And that's the truth.

Log the Truth

1. What excuses have you used to minimize personal responsibility? Did they work with others? With yourself?

2. Who has influenced your life for good? For bad? How did he or she do that?

3. In your own words, explain the quote, "Between stimulus and response is a place called choice."

4. What do you most like about making choices? What do you most dislike? Why?

Lie 11

Only Good Things Happen to Good People

The Truth about Trouble

E ach new day of the summer of 2002 seemed to bring a new abduction of a child by strangers. Many centered in our area of southern California, and their stories filled the newscasts. Although national statistics indicated that overall abductions had declined for several years, Americans didn't *feel* that way.

Our grandchildren spent a week with us, and on one of those rare occasions when a child's TV show wasn't on, we listened to an exception on the news: a local girl was rescued through the Amber Alert system, without having been molested or killed. In relief my wife said, "God was certainly with her, wasn't he?"

Hannah, our perceptive eight-year-old granddaughter then asked, "Does that mean God wasn't with the girls who were killed?"

Already she has tumbled onto the problem that perplexes theologians and common folk alike: How can you explain the pain and suffering of life if we have a loving God? Many genuinely struggle with that question. Ted Turner, known for his potshots at Christians, began by going to church and believing in God. But he abandoned faith after his sister, Mary Jane, died of a painful disease despite prayers that she be healed. "I was taught that God was love and God was powerful," Turner told *The New Yorker* magazine. "And I couldn't understand how someone so innocent should be made or allowed to suffer so."

Many believe that God provides a shield to keep pain, suffering, and trouble from his people. Hannah wondered about—and Turner is committed to—the lie that our faith will keep bad things from happening to us.

Identify the Lie

This lie has more than just a trace of truth. Like most lies, we can find enough truth to make it seem reasonable. I've always been drawn to Jesus' description of what he offers: "The thief comes only to steal and kill and destroy; I have come that they may have life, and have it to the full." The Revised Standard Version says, "...that they might have life and have it *abundantly*" (John 10:10, emphasis added).

Don't we all want a better life from being in Christ? Wouldn't we all love not being bothered by temptation, sickness, poverty, or trouble? Isn't that what having life "to the full" means? As usual, God's Word gives us the answers.

VICTORY OVER SPIRITUAL DEFEAT AND TEMPTATION

We have the promise of spiritual victory in our lives according to 1 John 4:4: "You, dear children, are from God and have overcome them, because the one who is in you is greater than the one who is in the world." "Them" refers to the opponents of God; we've already overcome them because *he* overcame them.

First Corinthians 10:13 clearly adds victory over temptation:

> No temptation has seized you except what is
> common to man. And God is faithful; he will not
> let you be tempted beyond what you can bear.
> But when you are tempted, he will also provide
> a way out so that you can stand up under it.

Awesome! We can beat temptation!

Victory over Sickness

"But he was pierced for our transgressions, he was crushed for our iniquities; the punishment that brought us peace was upon him, and *by his wounds we are healed*" (emphasis added). Many interpret Isaiah 53:5 to include that Christ's death on the cross also guarantees physical healing. If that interpretation is correct, then physical healing would be a promise God didn't keep for Turner's sister.

Victory over Poverty

And wouldn't we all enjoy material comfort and wealth? Read Malachi 3:10–11:

> "Bring the whole tithe into the storehouse, that there may be food in my house. Test me in this," says the LORD Almighty, "and see if I will not throw open the floodgates of heaven and pour out so much blessing that you will not have room enough for it. I will prevent pests from devouring your crops, and the vines in your fields will not cast their fruit," says the LORD Almighty.

Sounds like we won't have to worry financially if we tithe, right?

Victory over Difficulty

Let's extend victory to *whatever we desire*, as Jesus seems to say in John 14:13–14: "And I will do whatever you ask in my name, so that the Son may bring glory to the Father. You may ask me for anything in my name, and I will do it."

We merely ask for deliverance and protection, and we have them. That would certainly keep any random type of difficulty away, wouldn't it? How then can we explain the pain that genuine believers *do* experience?

A Bad Answer to a Good Question

Rabbi Harold Kushner tackled the issue in his classic book *When Bad Things Happen to Good People*. He considered two attributes of God: being both all-powerful and all-loving. He believes the existence of suffering contradicts the love of God, reasoning that if God were all-powerful, he would eliminate it. Kushner attempts to put us on the horns of a dilemma: Either God doesn't love us enough to banish suffering, or he's unable to.

Kushner chooses to sacrifice God's power; he'd prefer an impotent God to one that doesn't love us enough to eliminate suffering. Neither is particularly attractive nor biblical. But I learned long ago in a college logic class that when you're on the horns of a dilemma, you either break one of the horns or you find a third option, a path through the horns. In this case, we can do both. We call it the truth.

Learn the Truth

Rather than believing that Christianity will protect us from all difficulties, we discover the truth that hard times are real for all people. When we study this issue in the context of all the Bible says, we just can't reach the conclusion that Christians will never suffer. Let's examine three basic principles that develop that thought.

GOD'S WILL ISN'T ALWAYS DONE

If all that occurs was just what God wanted, then we could make an excellent case against the love of God. But when God gave us free will; he voluntarily limited his ability to carry out his will. What do we mean?

While I was pastoring my last church, the elders realized we needed to revise our entire structure to be both more biblical and more effective. They asked me to come up with some foundational principles and propose bylaws to support the changes. I did a great job. I tied in some material from the master's program in ministry I was then completing; I researched the structure and bylaws of numerous other churches; and I did a comprehensive study of what the Bible says about leadership and the local church.

What did the elders do? They changed it! Not entirely— they kept the bulk of the proposal—but they made some modifications. And I had some deep reservations about some of the adjustments (and not just because they were tweaking my ideas!). Although pastors are the biblically mandated leaders of the church, they don't always get their way! Others have a choice also.

My experience roughly corresponds to God's will. Yes, God has a desire for us, but he allows us to reject it. We saw that explained in greater detail in the last chapter, so let's just look at one passage that confirms it. "The Lord is not slow in keeping his promise, as some understand slowness. He is patient with you, not wanting anyone to perish, but everyone to come to repentance" (2 Peter 3:9).

At a minimum, this verse shows that we can't blame God for all that happens. Yes, God is all-powerful, but he chooses to not use his power to overcome our choices. So Kushner's assumption that God *isn't able* to end pain is incomplete. Genuine free will requires that God restrain himself at times. God's respect for our choices having consequences breaks one of the "horns of the dilemma."

TROUBLE IS TYPICAL

Rather than God's promising a life free from pain and suffering, he assures us that these qualities are a normal part of human existence. Why? Because Adam and Eve invited sin into the world, and we continue to provide accommodations for it. Sin always brings pain, suffering, and trouble. Every person, every Christian included, will experience that.

Jesus affirmed that trouble permeates the world and impacts believers in John 16:33: "I have told you these things, so that in me you may have peace. *In this world you will have trouble.* But take heart! I have overcome the world" (emphasis added).

Jesus' promise of trouble is lived out by faithful believers. Hebrews 11 begins with marvelous stories of people who experienced victories due to their faith. They "conquered kingdoms … shut the mouths of lions, quenched the fury of the flames, and escaped the edge of the sword … and routed foreign armies.

Women received back their dead, raised to life again" (vv. 33–35). That's the kind of spiritual life I yearn for, don't you? Conquering. Avoiding pain and suffering.

But we need to know the rest of the story, because it changes at the midpoint of verse 35.

> Others were tortured and refused to be released, so that they might gain a better resurrection. Some faced jeers and flogging, while still others were chained and put in prison. They were stoned; they were sawed in two; they were put to death by the sword. They went about in sheepskins and goatskins, destitute, persecuted and mistreated—the world was not worthy of them. They wandered in deserts and mountains, and in caves and holes in the ground. These were all commended for their faith, yet none of them received what had been promised (11:35-39).

The promise is deliverance. They didn't get it. Why? Did God not love them as much as the first group? Or was he powerful enough to deliver some, but then he ran out of power and couldn't deliver the others? Remember those questions; they're important, and we'll get back to them. But if trouble is a normal part of life, where does pain come from?

SOURCES OF PAIN

Up front, I certainly can't identify all pain with its source. Some troubles can be traced back; others can't. But understanding where suffering comes from can help us deal with it. Let's look at an incident in King David's life to show how different sources of pain can stem from a single event.

• Consequences of our Decisions

David couldn't blame God for the suffering in his life. In one incident, he made several choices that brought great difficulty and sorrow to many people.

One day David saw an attractive married woman, wallowed in his fantasies, and indulged his desires. The immediate consequence: she got pregnant. David quickly thought of a solution: He arranged for a seventy-two-hour leave for her military husband, sure that he'd sleep with her and that the child could be passed off as his.

Unfortunately, Uriah didn't feel right about enjoying the comforts of home while his fellow warriors still fought, and his loyalty signed the death warrant drawn up by David.

The next consequence: suffering. In 2 Samuel 12:9–10 we read:

> Why did you despise the word of the LORD by doing what is evil in his eyes? You struck down Uriah the Hittite with the sword and took his wife to be your own. You killed him with the sword of the Ammonites. Now, therefore, the sword will never depart from your house, *because* you despised me and took the wife of Uriah the Hittite to be your own (emphasis added).

Please don't miss the word I italicized: *because,* which indicates a cause/effect relationship. *Because* David acted violently, violence would follow him. You can read the rest of the book to learn the extent of suffering faced by David as a direct consequence of his actions. I think David realized he couldn't blame God, because David started the ball rolling. The rest just came along as a result of his choices.

• *Consequences of Others' Decisions*

On that same day, nearly 3,000 other people faced death. The promise of their future was stolen away, their families experienced significant loss, all because of the actions of others. Were these 3,000 to blame? Absolutely not. But they had to deal with suffering because the decisions of others had consequences.

David's choices affected millions of innocent people. Many people besides Bathsheba's baby and Uriah paid the price. Who knows how many soldiers as well as innocents lost their lives because of the violence that followed David the rest of his life? Not one of those people had a say in David's decision to commit adultery with Bathsheba. Not one of them deserved the suffering that followed.

Sometimes we can trace a clear and direct trail of our pain back to the decision of another person. Other times we can't identify the specific cause, except that somebody made a decision and others paid the price.

• Consequences of Life

Some pain can't be traced to any one incident. Why does a healthy nonsmoker get lung cancer? Why do tornados destroy one house and not another? Why does a mother die in a car accident while a drunk driver walks away unharmed? In my opinion, sometimes we can just be in the wrong place at the wrong time. Some might call this chance or coincidence. I just see it as part of life. When sin and decay entered a previously perfect world, bad consequences came along.

Among the numerous pets that composed the Riter household in my early years was Pete, a friendly, talkative, blue-and-white parakeet. He especially loved the evenings when he could come out of his cage and join the rest of the family. He'd fly from one person to another, perch on our water glasses to get a drink, and just enjoy being with us. My favorite trick was to get him on my finger, say, "Pete, give me a kiss," and watch him strut up my arm and bump my lips with his beak. Then I'd snap my fingers, and he'd strut back down. He was cool.

Despite all his talent, however, we could never potty train that darned bird. When Pete had to go, Pete went. Right there. We soon learned he meant absolutely nothing by it; it was neither criticism nor reward. (Birds can't control that function.) We just waited until it dried and flicked it off. (And in case you wonder if those flicks were ever directed at my sister, I plead the Fifth!)

Life is like bird droppings. Sometimes, we're just in the wrong place at the wrong time, and it drops on us. I think that's what Jesus was referring to in the following passage.

Now there were some present at that time who told Jesus about the Galileans whose blood Pilate had mixed with their sacrifices. Jesus answered, "Do you think that these Galileans were worse sinners than all the other Galileans because they suffered this way? I tell you, no! But unless you repent, you too will all perish. Or those eighteen who died when the tower in Siloam fell on them—do you think they were more guilty than all the others living in Jerusalem? I tell you, no! But unless you repent, you too will all perish" (Luke 13:1-5).

Jesus intentionally directed the source of these disasters away from the victims. His solution to pain? Don't look backward to blame. Be sure you're right with God, and look ahead to avoid the worst disaster—hell.

Let's look at one more source of pain, one that may change the way we look at trials.

• Consequences of Testing

While I was in graduate school, one professor surprised me by saying he hated to give tests. He disliked making some students feel bad with a poor grade, when they'd truly done the work but just didn't take tests well. Even though I told him I agreed with him, he continued to test us despite his dislike of the process. Now that I'm a professor at the same university, my opinion has changed.

I like tests. Now, I don't like taking the time to build one, and I'd rather not grade them. But if nothing else, they show me if I've done a good job teaching! More importantly, they also reveal if the students have grasped the concepts of the course. I've learned God does the same thing.

Blessed is the man who perseveres under *trial*, because when he has stood the *test*, he will receive the crown of life that God has promised to those who love him. When *tempted*, no one should say, "God is tempting me." For God cannot be tempted by evil, nor does he tempt anyone … (James 1:12–13, emphasis added).

Look at those three words: *trial, test,* and *tempted.* In the original language, they have the same root; it basically means "to pierce." A trial is an event that "pierces" our lives and disrupts us. Pain and suffering may be there. Satan may use the trial as a *temptation;* but God may also use the same trial as a *test.*

When God tests us, he provides a way for us to learn where we are in relationship to him.

He wants us to see areas in our lives we need to strengthen, steps we can take to avoid sin, and opportunities to lean on his understanding. That doesn't mean God necessarily causes the pain, he merely used it as a life check.

Now, here's where I must confess something: I have no wisdom, no method, no surefire way to identify the source of all the pain we experience in life. Sometimes we can discover its source; sometimes we cannot. When we can, we are grateful, and the hard times seem a bit easier to bear. When we can't, we simply have to trust that God loves us and that he is good.

Live the Truth

Rather than accepting the lie that pain is evidence of God's lack of either love or power, we can live in the truth.

EMBRACE THE PRIVILEGE OF PAIN

I can't help but recall some definitions a college professor gave me, "A masochist says, 'Hurt me.' A sadist says, 'No.'" Fortunately, I'm neither. I don't like pain; I don't seek it; and I don't want to cause pain to others. I would much prefer the total absence of temptation, pain, and suffering. But God, in his love, encourages us to see that suffering includes redemption.

But *rejoice that you participate in the sufferings of Christ,* so that you may be overjoyed when his glory is revealed. If you are insulted because of the name of Christ, you are blessed, for the Spirit of glory and of God rests on you. If you suffer, it should not be as a murderer or thief or any other kind of criminal, or even as a meddler. However, if you suffer as a Christian, do not be ashamed, but praise God that you bear that name (1 Peter 4:13–16, emphasis added).

Suffering as a *privilege*? Come on, God. That doesn't make sense to most of us. Why should we rejoice? Because when we suffer as believers, we confirm that we indeed *are* believers. I'm convinced that one of Satan's operating principles is to "let sleeping Christians lie." If we're doing nothing for God, Satan has no need to stir us up by making life difficult. Why would he want to take the chance we may grow in our faith? So suffering we receive because of our faith indicates we have some.

SEE PAIN REDEEMED IN US

James the brother of Christ moves the redemption of suffering even further along.

Consider it pure joy, my brothers, whenever you face trials of many kinds, because you know that the testing of your faith develops perseverance. Perseverance must finish its work so that you may be mature and complete, not lacking anything (James 1:2–4, emphasis added).

When we face any kind of trial, we are to rejoice. Any trials. Not just those that affirm our faith. Those with no known purpose. Those that result from evil choices. Those that come from other people's decisions. We are to meet all of those with joy.

Verses three and four tell us why joy amid trials is so important. James says it's part of a process that helps us become "mature and complete, not lacking anything."

God's bringing us to this spiritual maturity is certainly an expression of his love for us. Think back to Kushner's proposition that suffering contradicts the love of God. Does it? Only if God doesn't involve himself. If we feel pain, and God ignores it, then we can accuse him of a lack of love. But he doesn't leave us alone. He wants the best for us, and he actively works so that we can achieve it. One of the tools he uses can be suffering.

SEE PAIN REDEEMED IN THE SITUATION

God also demonstrates how his power can bring good from the worst of situations. My first senior pastorate combined great joys with great frustration. I never considered leaving the ministry, but I knew where and how I ministered would certainly change. Those were three very tough years. Yet looking back offers a clear picture that God was always present and working. In a church that averaged ninety in attendance when I started, we had fifty decisions for Christ in just one year. People took the demands of God seriously and were challenged to grow deeper in their faith. As I mentioned before, my stepdaughter met a local man, married him, and my wife and I now have two fantastic grandchildren. Just last week I had breakfast with a former member of the church who's remained a good friend over the years.

After we left there, God led us to start a new church in the nearby town of Temecula, the most fulfilling and joyful ministry of my life. We still live here, loving the mountains that surround our valley, the morning mist that burns away in the bright sun, the clean air, vineyards, and easy access to both the mountains and the beach.

Were those three years painful? Without a doubt. Did suffering exist? Absolutely. But the previous two paragraphs detail just some of the very good things God accomplished through a painful experience. I learned the truth of Romans 8:28: "We *know* that in *all things God works for the good* of those who love him and are called according to his purpose" (emphasis added).

God shows his power by always working for good in the most evil situations. In our naiveté, let's not deny the reality of evil and pain. They exist, and they hurt! But God doesn't leave us alone. He works for good and sometimes, perhaps more often than we know, he softens the blows so the trials and tests of life don't hurt quite so much.

I'm amazed at God's power: He fully allows every person on earth to make free choices even when those choices are sinful and evil. He allows damaging consequences, and he still brings good to the situation and good to us. I guess Kushner missed the truth, didn't he? Pain doesn't negate God's love and power, it demonstrates them. And that's the truth.

Log the Truth

1. Have you believed that faith will keep you from trouble? Did your belief match reality?

2. How does Jesus' promise of trouble (see John 16:33) affect you?

3. Have your choices brought pain to your life? Describe one event.

4. Have others' choices brought pain to your life? Describe one event.

5. Have circumstances brought pain to your life? Describe one event.

6. How has God used any of this pain to work for good—in you or in others?

7. Describe a time when you "embraced pain" and saw God redeem it.

Lie 12

We Have the Truth
The Truth about Unity

I received the brochure in the mail and almost cried. The new church being advertised was purpose driven, relevant, contemporary, and had a clear mission statement. Except for one factor, it sounded like a church I would love to attend. Look at some key phrases from the flyer, and see if you recognize the source of my grief.

> People avoid church for all kinds of reasons. Too often church services are boring, there's too much talk about money, and the music is lame. Times and styles change and … we don't think church should feel like you're stuck in a time warp. We are starting the kind of church you've been looking for: Real, Radical, Relevant, and Relational! Our services feature modern music, today's technology, genuine people, blue jeans, and positive messages that address the issues you face in today's world. People are finding that church can be interesting, friendly, spiritually relevant, and, dare we say it? Fun! But if you're looking for hard pews, sleepy hymns, boring

sermons, empty rituals, and a huge offering plate
… sorry. We can't please everyone.

What semi-hidden message did this church convey? Avoid other churches. Other churches will bore you and beg for your money. They have lame music and harder pews. But, *we* do church right.

Too often we think our group has a lock on the truth. We're certain we're more faithful than other churches. Other churches possess significant flaws, but not our church. And we fall victim to the lie: our church is the best.

Identify the Lie

I'm amazed at the prevalence of the "we have the truth and you don't" lie. I've received dozens of flyers from new churches, and too many echo the one I quoted earlier. (I almost wonder if some wounded pastor sits in his office and writes this text for all new churches!) And, aren't we all tempted to do something similar? We enjoy our church and invite Christians who faithfully attend other fellowships to join us. "Pastor Matt gives such funny messages!" "Our praise team takes me straight to heaven—you should hear them." "When Lynn plays the organ I feel like I hear angels singing."

Most congregational growth comes from Christians moving from one church to another, not from people becoming believers. We don't mind that, do we? After all, our church does it right. We criticize other denominations because they don't see faith quite the way we do. Charismatics sometimes wonder if non-charismatics really have a solid faith. And non-charismatics have the same question about charismatics. The Mormon Church arose because the founder, Joseph Smith, couldn't figure out which Christian group he should join. Each one he investigated said the *others* were wrong while *they* were right.

Churches have problems. I've seen more than my share, and if you've spent more than thirty minutes in one, you probably have as well. In no way do I recommend we ignore problems, but do we have to run other believers down to make our church look better? Doesn't our critical spirit imply that we compete with one another? Criticism and competition never foster unity; they only drive the body of Christ apart. Disunity arises from three basic lies: Everybody else has to believe like us, behave like us, and belong to us. We allow untruth to damage us when we believe that unity comes from any of these.

BELIEVING LIKE US

Our stepdaughter once attended a church whose bylaws required each member to accept the pretribulation, premillenial view of end times. That's certainly one of the basic viewpoints, but it's not the only one. Except for that church. Until recently, a major denomination wouldn't allow its pastors to participate in a worship event with other Christians from other denominations. Their rationale? Involvement in the event would dilute *their* witness that they had the truth about the Christian experience. Worshiping with others implied that the others might have some truth in areas of disagreement.

The Bible clearly contradicts the lie that unity comes from full agreement on all doctrinal issues, so we know this struggle is nothing new. The early church grappled with such important doctrinal issues as whether or not Christians should eat meat. Nearly all the meat sold in the market had been sacrificed to idols, so did eating meat involve you in idol worship? Should Christians only eat vegetables to avoid even the appearance of idolatry? Speaking of worship, on which day of the week should Christians gather? On the Jewish Sabbath or on Sunday, to honor the day of Christ's resurrection? Those on each side of these issues looked down on believers on the other. Look at the truth in Romans 14:1-6:

> Accept him whose faith is weak, *without passing judgment* on disputable matters. One man's faith allows him to eat everything, but another man, whose faith is weak, eats only vegetables. The man who eats everything must not look down on him who does not, and the man who does not eat everything must not

condemn the man who does, for God has accepted him. Who are you to judge someone else's servant? To his own master he stands or falls. And he will stand, for the Lord is able to make him stand.

One man considers one day more sacred than another; another man considers every day alike. Each one should be fully convinced in his own mind. He who regards one day as special, does so to the Lord. He who eats meat, eats to the Lord, for he gives thanks to God; and he who abstains, does so to the Lord and gives thanks to God (emphasis added).

Worship and avoiding idolatry touch on the heart of faith. Christians disagreed, and Scripture says that was acceptable! We don't build our unity on agreeing on all the issues. Different opinions can be held. Later we'll examine where to draw the line, but thinking we must agree on all issues is believing a lie.

BEHAVING LIKE US

Christians have become famous—or infamous—for selecting certain behaviors that identify us as good believers, as part of the right group. To some, handling poisonous snakes, according to Mark 16:18 marks true faith. Those who prefer to let sleeping snakes lie lack true faith. I grew up in a church that followed the practice of the early church (Acts 20:7) by observing communion each week. That clearly distinguished us from other churches that weren't as "faithful" to the New Testament example.

At various times in American history, some churches required certain behaviors such as avoiding all alcohol or not attending movies as clear signs that they were in the right group. Does this principle of establishing unity match the biblical standard? Let's look again at Romans 14 for our answer.

He who regards one day as special, does so to the Lord. He who eats meat, eats to the Lord, for he gives thanks to God; and he who abstains, does so to the Lord and gives thanks to God. For none of us lives to himself alone and none of us dies to himself alone. If we live, we live to the Lord; and if we die, we die to the Lord. So, whether we live or die, *we belong to the Lord* (vv. 6–8, emphasis added).

Despite different behaviors on the issues of eating meat and worshiping on a particular day, both sides still belonged to the Lord. The importance of these issues didn't transcend the inherent unity between believers. Their unity extended beyond behavior.

BELONGING TO US

Several Christian groups have believed that only one church exists in a city—theirs. So, if you're not in their group, you're not anywhere. Their group exclusively has the truth. I've told the story of an aunt whose son quit going to church, and a neighbor invited him to join them for breakfast and church. He hadn't gone in years and decided to do it. His mom was incensed at the neighbor for taking her son to a church outside her denomination. She'd rather he not go at all than attend another group.

In 1 Corinthians 1:2 God extends the scope of true believers far beyond being in one particular group: "To the church of God in Corinth, to those sanctified in Christ Jesus and called to be holy, *together with all those everywhere who call on the name of our Lord Jesus Christ*—their Lord and ours ..." (emphasis added).

Pretty clear, isn't it? The church of God includes all those everywhere who call on the name of our Lord Jesus Christ. No one geographical or denominational group can claim that they alone are the church.

So, what's the truth about the source of unity between believers?

Learn the Truth

We begin our search for the truth by examining God's perspective on unity.

UNITY'S VALUE TO GOD

We've seen that God offers us great freedom on matters of opinion. God doesn't base unity on full agreement. But some issues are essential, and we must find unity in that camp, according to Ephesians 4:3: "Make every effort to keep the unity of the Spirit through the bond of peace."

Notice that the verse says, "keep the unity." God gives us unity; we don't create it. Our job is to maintain it, and that job is vital. In the original language, the phrase "make every effort" is active, in the present tense, and imperative. Active means we must do something, we can't just sit passively. The present tense means that we do something now, and that we *keep* doing it. We don't make just one or two attempts, find them difficult, and quit. Imperative equates to a command. It's not a suggestion, and that takes this beyond a matter that we can justifiably disagree on.

God wills that his children be united. It's non-negotiable. The normal Christian life has believers passionately working to keep and increase our unity. Unity possesses an intrinsic value to God for us. But unity's importance goes a step further. Unity is necessary to carry out the mission of the church.

UNITY'S VALUE FOR MISSION

I attended the Promise Keepers' Clergy Conference in Atlanta back in 1996. Max Lucado brought out two dimensions I had never seen in a very familiar text. In Jesus' "Last Will and Testament," he laid out kingdom values, goals, and strategies. John 17:20–23 takes center stage.

> My prayer is not for them alone. I pray also for those who will believe in me through their message, that all of them may be one, Father, just as you are in me and I am in you. May they also be in us *so that the world may believe* that you

have sent me. I have given them the glory that you gave me, that they may be *one as we are one*: I in them and you in me. May they be brought to *complete unity* to let the world know that you sent me and have loved them even as you have loved me (emphasis added).

First, think about the *degree of unity* Jesus desires. Jesus wants us to be united in the same manner that he and the Father are. The next sentence defines that as complete unity. Lucado provided the tool for tremendous conviction—I've never seen or even desired that type of unity with other followers of Jesus. Cooperate, yes. Love others, absolutely. But maintaining a divine level of unity greatly infringes on my individuality and choice. I don't particularly like that. But Jesus does, and he's Lord. We all need to carefully consider this very clear command and description of unity that Jesus wants for us. If we embrace it, that unity will change our lives from the core.

Second, think about the strategic role of unity, according to Jesus. He wants us to be one "so that the world may believe." Yes, the church has grown over the centuries. But 1900 years after Jesus gave us the mission of bringing the world to God, most of the world hasn't come to Christ. Could our lack of unity be part of the reason people are going to hell? I think that's what Jesus tells us. Apart from Jesus commanding our unity, we can't obey his other command to reach the world. People can understandably reject Christ when his followers can't even get along.

And what followers must we be united with? "All those everywhere who call upon the name of our Lord Jesus Christ." Doesn't that phrase echo the verse we read earlier from 1 Corinthians 1:2? Apparently, Jesus requires an observable, intense, passionate unity between all believers before we can effectively reach the world.

We, however, would rather gather in our holy huddles, in our "right" group, criticize other Christians, live separately from them, and wonder why people won't come to Christ. I think we can stop wondering.

UNITY'S SOURCES

Before we discover how to live out the truth of unity, we must understand the sources. Jesus said we've already been given them, so let's discover what we unite around.

• *The Person of Jesus*

Think back again to 1 Corinthians 1:2, which says all people everywhere who call on Jesus make up the church. The John passage amplifies that truth when Jesus reveals the source of our unity in verse 23: "*I in them* and you in me" (emphasis added). Being in Christ is what unites us. Simple, isn't it? This observable unity is to extend to all believers. If we share Jesus, we are united. Period. And we need to act like it.

If we share him, we don't have to believe all the same things, behave in the same ways, or belong to the same specific group. We don't all have to take communion each week, or on the first Sunday, or the fifth. We don't all have to believe in postmillennialism. We don't all have to belong to the same church or denomination. We don't all have to agree on whether James and Jude were brothers or cousins of Jesus. Like them, we're already united through him. That's a hard fact.

Obviously, we must share the Jesus of the Bible, not the creation of someone who claims to have seen an angel and gives this creature the name of Jesus. Tim Rice is a great composer, but Tim Riter is a different person, even though we share the same first name and our last names are pretty close. There is only one Savior and Lord named Jesus.

• *Essential Beliefs*

The second source of unity focuses on essential beliefs. We must agree on core truths about God, Jesus, and faith. Thomas Jefferson expressed the needed distinction between core truth and opinion: "In matters of principle, stand like a rock. In matters of taste, swim with the current." Great advice, but how do we know which beliefs are core?

Let's go back to Ephesians 4:3, where we're commanded to maintain our unity. That command leads to seven core doctrinal beliefs that unite us (vv. 4-6): "There is *one body* and *one Spirit*—just as you were called to *one hope* when you were called—*one Lord, one faith, one baptism; one God* and Father of all, who is over all and through all and in all" (emphasis added).

God knew what he was doing when he mentioned these "ones" immediately after the unity command. Holding on to them ensures that we accurately follow the biblical Jesus. Let's look at each one separately.

> •*One body* refers to the church, that group of people united in Jesus. This invalidates the common idea of solitary Christians who don't connect with other believers.

> •*One Spirit* brings in the reality of the Holy Spirit as part of the Godhead, fully God in every way.

> •*One hope* looks to the future return of Christ and our home in heaven.

> •*One Lord* establishes Jesus Christ as both part of the Godhead and the boss of our lives, that we give him his rightful place as number one.

> •*One faith* proclaims that belief in Jesus, not being good or believing the correct doctrine, brings us into a relationship.

> •*One baptism* speaks to the need to enter into that relationship, that one doesn't automatically become a Christian because your parents were.

> •*One God and Father* presents him as preeminent in the Trinity.

These seven core truths provide the foundation for unity. Complete doctrinal agreement doesn't seem to be necessary, but accord on key essentials that the Bible links to unity certainly is.

Now, does a person need a clear understanding of each "one" before coming to Christ? No, just that we sin, we're guilty, and we need to accept Jesus as our Lord and Savior. The rest comes with growth.

How can we determine if an aberrant group is within the kingdom or not? We apply these core beliefs.

But what about those that profess to agree with these foundational doctrines, but their behavior doesn't bear out their words? Although non-commanded specific behavior doesn't unite us, a refusal to obey God's clear commands after we come to faith may very well pull us apart.

• Obedient Faith

After ten years of marriage, Chet began a series of affairs. He showed no remorse, no desire to change. He offered Cindy the opportunity to stay with him but said, "Cindy, I cherish what we have, but I just don't want to eliminate other women in my life; they bring me something special. I'd like to keep things just as they are now. I hope that's fine with you."

Understandably, Cindy knew that Chet had shattered their unity, saw nothing wrong, and had no desire to change his behavior. Chet destroyed their marriage bond. He didn't desire any real kind of unity between Cindy and him.

Our behavior can break unity in the church as well. And although behavior doesn't create unity, unrepentant, continued, serious sin certainly can break it. Paul illustrated that in 1 Corinthians 5. He began with an example in verses 1–5, and then gave the principle in verses 9–13. We find the core in verses 11–13.

> I am writing you that you *must not associate* with anyone who calls himself a brother but is sexually immoral or greedy, an idolater or a slanderer, a drunkard or a swindler. With such a man do not even eat. What business is it of mine to judge those outside the church? Are you not to judge those inside? God will judge those outside. "*Expel the wicked man from among you*" (emphasis added).

Please understand that we're neither saved nor united by our behavior. But a genuine faith includes obedience, according to James 2:21–24.

> Was not our ancestor Abraham considered righteous for what he did when he offered his son Isaac on the altar? You see that his faith and his actions were working together, and his faith was made complete by what he did. And the scripture was fulfilled that says, "Abraham believed God, and it was credited to him as righteousness," and he was called God's friend. You see that a person is justified by what he does and not by faith alone.

Unrepentant, continued, serious sin can break the unity between brothers and sisters in the church. Behavior affects people. Behavior can break bonds. So if we desire unity, we need to act in ways that advance it.

Live the Truth

Understanding the essentiality of unity mandates that we change in how we live out our faith. Several years ago, Ted Haggard began a new church in Colorado Springs, and after a rocky beginning they began to grow significantly. Another church in the area felt threatened and attacked them publicly and repeatedly. Haggard had committed himself to unity between churches, but he didn't have a clue on how to heal this breach.

Then he learned that the other church was having difficulty paying their mortgage of about $100,000. He prayed, talked to his advisors, and took a check for $100,000 to the other pastor. What an amazing act of unity! Like Haggard did, let's move beyond our intellectual understanding of unity, and make it practical.

ACCEPT UNITY

I spoke on unity at my last church, yearning to stretch my people just a little. One response staggered me. Paul Falkenstein, one of our newer people, wrote, "If someone would ask me tomorrow what the name of my (family's) church was, can I say 'We are members of the church in San Pedro that belongs to Jesus Christ' without worrying about the possibility of my individual church being lost to anonymity? Should I care?"

Paul went on to explore concepts such as placing denominational loyalty below living in harmony with all fellow believers, or even merging some congregations to more effectively serve Christ in a certain community. I felt both threatened and thrilled! Practicing the kind of unity Jesus has with the Father will threaten our "acceptable" ways of doing things. It will also thrill us as we see our connection to the greater body of Christ. Let's accept unity as a foundational principle from God.

SPEAK UNITY

At a minimum, unity requires that we lift up other churches in how we speak about them. The command in Ephesians 4:29 extends beyond individuals to congregations: "Do not let any unwholesome talk come out of your mouths, but only what is helpful for building others up according to their needs, that it may benefit those who listen."

The verse doesn't tell us to ignore problems; it simply exhorts us to praise other congregations, other groups of believers. Occasionally we've had visitors in our church who were clearly uncomfortable with our style of worship. It's my pleasure to recommend another local church where they might feel more at home. Another church in the Temecula area advertises itself as "one of the many great churches in our valley." I like that! Their ad shows that we can mention our strengths without mentioning others' weaknesses.

Let's all commit to praising other Christian churches and avoiding negative statements. The world needs to know that we really do like and admire one another.

WORK UNITY

We cannot limit unity to an abstract principle, to an esoteric bond between all Christians, or even positive words among believers. Just as the unity between the Father and the

Son determines how they behave, so does our unity within the body of Christ. What follows are some examples of unity in practice. Some are radical; some are simply common sense. Some have been done; some are dreams. But be willing to think outside the stained glass in order to let the Holy Spirit lead you and those around you into a deeper unity.

•In San Pedro, twenty-five local churches closed their doors one Sunday morning to worship as "the church of San Pedro." We called the event "San Pedro Celebrates Christ"— and we truly did. That day played a role in changing the churches in that community. Churches have worked together to evaluate how their unique identity fits within the greater Christian community. Various united evangelistic thrusts have resulted.

•More than sixty churches in Colorado Springs have come together, hired a coordinator, and cooperate in a number of events to impact the community for Christ.

•We mentioned earlier about how one church financially helped another very different congregation financially. If our church is blessed with worship leaders or musicians, could we perhaps send some to a church that needs some?

•Granite Hills Christian Church, part of the independent Christian churches, began talking to First Christian Church in El Cajon, CA, from the Disciples of Christ denomination. They discovered they shared many beliefs and wanted to extend their impact on the community. They talked about uniting, researched what worked and what didn't, and finally combined into one new church that became more effective than either was before.

One last question: If Jesus cares so much about our unity, shouldn't we? Shouldn't we begin to carefully strategize on how to express that unity? How we might change to express it even more? Is Jesus' desire for our unity perhaps more important than our preference to remain isolated from one another?

You see, we need a dynamic unity with other Christians. We need that to obey Jesus. We need that to reach people for Christ. We need that to become mature believers. And that's the truth.

Log the Truth

1. Have you ever felt separated from other church congregations who also love Jesus?

2. What might be the sources of those feelings of separation?

3. Do you think it's possible for believers to achieve the level of unity desired by Jesus (see John 17:20–22)? Have you ever experienced it? Explain.

4. If you desire godly unity, what keeps you from reaching it?

5. Has your loyalty to your local church or denomination lessened your unity with all believers? How can you balance loyalty to each of these?

6. What can you do in the next month to advance this goal of unity?

Epilogue:

Released by the Truth:

The Truth about Finding Lies

The full moon shone almost like daylight at the church camp in the mountains above Pasadena and provided an opportunity I couldn't resist. "Rhonda, don't stay out too long here at night; you might get moon burn." (This happened back in the mid 1960s, before we knew much about skin cancer. Sunscreen didn't exist, and all teens wanted a bronze tan.)

"Moon burn? What's that?" Although an "A" student, Rhonda had developed a well-earned reputation for gullibility.

"Well, you know moonlight is just reflected sunlight, but the reflection takes away the part of the rays that cause a tan. So, instead of these rays making you darker, they cause your tan to fade."

She bought it and stayed out of the moonlight—until our laughter let her know she'd been had. Again. The rest of the week she went by the nickname, "Miss Moon Burn."

Karl possessed one of the gentlest spirits I've ever encountered. He was gracious, thoughtful, and considerate—except in elders' meetings. With a gift of seeing any possible flaw in any proposal, Karl consistently took an opposing position. He saw flaws both imagined and invisible. He questioned the reasons and motives for an idea. He questioned the evidence used to support a concept. His attitude remained nice, but he took a contrary position on everything.

Rhonda and Karl represent the polar opposites of testing ideas. Rhonda cultivated gullibility into an art form: She accepted anything that anyone said. Karl cultivated questioning to an art form: He disagreed with anything that anyone said.

Ideas new to us confront us with great frequency. Mistruths and misconceptions abound. There are ways, though to test ideas for their truthfulness. We can learn how to avoid the extremes of Rhonda and Karl.

Back in high school days, our pastor encouraged us to verify what he said. He didn't want us to blindly trust him. "Whatever I say, check it out. Be sure it matches the Bible, that it makes sense." Lester Ragland took that concept straight from the New Testament.

While taking the message of Jesus to the towns of his world, Paul came to Berea, and went to the synagogue there. The people's dual response is perfect: "… they received the message with great eagerness and examined the Scriptures every day to see if what Paul said was true" (Acts 17:11).

The Bereans had an open attitude, but wanted to check out what was being communicated. Paul *said* this Jesus was the Messiah promised in the Old Testament, so they compared what Paul said to what God had said. A wise decision.

Check It Out

Like the people Paul taught, we need to commit to the ongoing process of examining all of our beliefs, values, and opinions through the filter of Scripture. Add to that our own quirks, what we're taught by pastors and others, and ideas that pop up in small groups. We don't want to be obnoxious, but we do want the freedom that comes with knowing the truth, the whole truth, and nothing but the truth.

If we truly desire to grow in Christ, we need to distinguish between beliefs that will help us grow and beliefs that will hinder our growth. How do we make that distinction? Well, unless we check out everything, we may miss a crucial untruth.

Look at the process in 1 Thessalonians 5:21-22:"Test everything. Hold on to the good. Avoid every kind of evil."

The second two sentences in the passage provide our growth goal: to grab onto good and to avoid evil. The first sentence provides our method: to test *everything*. Unless we can tell what's good and what's evil, we can't hold on to or avoid anything. We test the material in this book. We test what our pastors say. We test what our small group leaders say. We test what our friends say. We test our own beliefs and values.

Does testing everything mean that we suspend all beliefs until we check everything out first? Obviously not. We don't get bogged down evaluating too many subjects at once, or we'll just get confused and finish few! We check out one issue at a time. Here's a way to prioritize and clarify the process:

First, we check *time-critical issues*. Some concepts require timeliness. If our church discusses whether to maintain traditional worship or transition to contemporary worship, then we need to first check out our beliefs and values on the purpose and mission of the church, how the church should balance ministry to existing members and to prospective members, and worship itself. If a crisis comes up, we study what the Bible teaches on that. If a friend camps on a doctrinal issue that we wonder about, then we explore it.

Second, we check *significant issues*. Some subjects don't carry a lot of weight, others do. Our beliefs about who God is will shape how we interpret everything else, so we probably should deal with these before determining if we should serve communion from just one cup, as Jesus did.

Third, we *listen to God's leading*. Some issues will rise to the surface just before the time of need, so be sensitive. Some years ago the topic of church discipline caught my attention, although nothing in the church seemed to cause that. I enjoyed the study I did, and within a few months, a situation came up where discipline applied. God had given me a heads up.

Fourth, we *revisit previous studies* as we continue to learn and grow. I regularly refine my ideas about the person of God. Now, I've never been heretical; don't get me wrong! But I've discovered that some truths build on one another. I had some early beliefs on spiritual gifts, mostly based on what I'd long been taught. I questioned the logical support of some of my earlier conclusions and studied the subject intensely. Based on what I learned, I had to revise my original beliefs. Later, I went into greater depth in learning about the Trinity, and I found I had to again revise my conclusions about spiritual gifts.

I encourage you to stay open. Don't get too locked into a set of beliefs that shut the door on new insights God may bring. You probably won't make wholesale changes, just revisions. But each revision, if biblically based, brings you closer to the full truth. And that's good.

Check the Source

I've found that the source of ideas can be as important as the ideas themselves. I follow professional football and enjoy a good Super Bowl party. What I like better than all the goodies, though, is trying to figure out who'll win the game. No one does that better than Hank Stram, former coach of the Kansas City Chiefs and currently a football commentator. He developed a system that's predicted something like eighteen out of the last nineteen Super Bowl winners.

When Stram chose the New England Patriots over the St. Louis Rams for the 2002 Super Bowl, I paid attention. Some of my friends picked the Rams and gave good reasons for their choice. Other friends picked the Patriots and gave good reasons for their choice as well. Before I made my own prediction, I considered the sources. None of my friends had the expertise or track record of Stram. Even though I rooted for my Rams, I knew they'd be in trouble. They were. The ultimate source for pigskin prognostication proved right again.

Picking a Super Bowl winner isn't really a heavy-duty spiritual decision, but how do we verify the source when we do have a question of faith or values?

First, is the person *authoritative*? I don't mean he must have an earned Ph.D. in theology, but does he know his stuff? Does she have some spiritual maturity, or does she jump on the latest new idea? Does he study an issue or just express his opinions? Rick Warren says opinions are like noses: Everyone has one. I disagree; opinions are more like fingers and toes: everyone has at least two and may have many more. We've all known people who live by the slogan, "My mind is made up; don't confuse me with the facts."

Second, what are the person's *biases*? We all have them. But to evaluate a source (and this includes evaluating our own beliefs!), we need to know where those biases come from. Charismatic, non-charismatic, or anti-charismatic? Arminian or Calvinist? Traditionalist or progressive? Theologically liberal or conservative? Gullible or contrary? A thinker or a feeler? Positive or negative church experiences?

A person's biases don't show whether or not that person has the truth, but knowing the belief system of our source helps us in evaluation. And if a person *speaks against* his or her interest or bias, then we pay more attention.

Third, is the person *reliable*? Does she usually come out on the correct side, like Stram does with Super Bowl winners? Or does he match the guy who in 1987 wrote *88 Reasons the Rapture Will Happen in 1988*. The year 1988 ended with no rapture that I noticed. Next he wrote *89 Reasons the Rapture Will REALLY Happen in 1989*. That guy dropped out of sight in early 1990. He wasn't a reliable source.

Once we apply these standards to the sources of ideas, we then go to the ideas themselves.

Check the Message

Before we can ever apply the content of a message to a standard, we must *have* a standard. Fortunately, we can check truth with the Source of truth: God and his Word.

The NIV records seventy-eight times when Jesus began his remarks by saying, "I tell you the truth." Why did he value truth so much? He said truth summarizes his own nature: "*I am* the way and *the truth* and the life" (John 14:6, emphasis added).

Jesus also identified the third person of the Trinity as truth: "But when he, the *Spirit of truth*, comes, he will guide you into all truth" (John 16:13, emphasis added). Quoting David, Jesus spoke from the cross and identified his Father as truth:"Into your hands I commit my spirit; redeem me, O LORD, *the God of truth*" (Psalm 31:5, emphasis added).

Jesus knew that the words of God contained truth: "Sanctify them by the truth; *your word is truth*" (John 17:17, emphasis added).

And finally, Jesus recognized Satan as the opposite of truth:

> You belong to your father, *the devil*, and you want to carry out your father's desire. He was a murderer from the beginning, not holding to the truth, for there is no truth in him. When he lies, he speaks his native language, for he is a liar and the *father of lies* (John 8:44, emphasis added).

Jesus was very clear about each member of the Trinity being a source of truth. Later in the New Testament, Paul affirms the Bible as an authoritative source of God's truth:"*All Scripture is God-breathed* and is useful for teaching, rebuking, correcting and training in righteousness, so that the man of God may be *thoroughly equipped* for every good work" (2 Timothy 3:16–17, emphasis added).

To summarize, God the Father, God the Son, and God the Spirit are all identified with truth. So is God's Word. That means, we must examine the truthfulness of any of our beliefs in light of God's Word, not our preferences, not what we've long been taught, not what our pastor says, not what benefits us.

Now, let's look at three questions we can use to evaluate the truthfulness of any message.

1. Is it consistent with the entire witness of the Bible? Keep this slogan in mind:"A text without a context is a pretext." Linking the context with the words of the passage or verse helps us avoid "proof-texting," pulling one verse out of context to prove a point. The broader the context; the greater the understanding.

Writing my second book provided one of my greatest challenges. I wanted *A Passionate Pursuit of God* to present the awesome privilege we have of knowing God as well as to give practical steps to do that. At first, I was quite intimidated by the task. How do you summarize the transcendent Creator of the universe in 150 pages? How do you blend brevity and accuracy? I started by using my computer Bible search program to discover every verse in the Bible that dealt with knowing God or Jesus. Every one. I didn't mention all those verses in the book, but I used every one in my thinking and writing. I didn't ignore a single verse. Why? I wanted to pass on truth about knowing God. I didn't want any of my words to contradict or confuse even one verse of Scripture. I wanted to express truth.

All of us need to do the same with our own beliefs and values. We can use computer Bible programs, topical Bibles, concordances, good commentaries, and wise advice, but we need to be thorough.

One of my great frustrations comes from how we address such issues as whether or not women should be pastors in the church. We usually hear one side using some verses, and the other side using other verses. We need to find a way to put all the verses together! We don't discover truth with dueling verses! Who has the most? Who has the best? If all Scripture is true, then it won't contradict itself. We need to understand all that God said about the subject before holding on too tightly to a conclusion.

2. Is the message consistent with historical under-standing? I don't mean that "tradition" stands on the same level of authority with God's Word! The phrase "If it's new, it isn't true" summarizes a generally wise approach—if we don't take it too far. But if the "new idea" contradicts the historical understanding, then realize that the burden of proof lies with those proposing the new slant. If the idea is true, that can be done.

The historical church hasn't always believed only the truth. Martin Luther proved that. More recently, some churches taught racism and bigotry. Overcoming these teachings required changes in our understanding of truth.

Take the time to cautiously evaluate "new" ideas, but remember that as long ago as Solomon's time people recognized "There is nothing new under the sun" (Ecclesiastes 1:9). Methods frequently change, but principles never do.

3. Is the message important enough to be considered an "essential" truth? Is this a hill you're willing to die on? Or is it something that Christians can validly disagree on, and still be solid Christians and love one another? Too often we've battled and separated over different interpretations of "truth," when in reality we separated over opinion. Paul warns us against that in Romans 14:1-3:

> Accept him whose faith is weak, without passing judgment on disputable matters. One man's faith allows him to eat everything, but another man, whose faith is weak, eats only vegetables. The man who eats everything must not look down on him who does not, and the man who does not eat everything must not condemn the man who does, for God has accepted him.

As a general indicator of doctrinal essentials we must believe, Ephesians 4 says it all. (See Lie 12 for a more complete discussion of the passage.)

> Make every effort to keep the unity of the Spirit through the bond of peace. There is one body and one Spirit—just as you were called to one hope when you were called—one Lord, one faith, one baptism; one God and Father of all, who is over all and through all and in all (vv.3-6).

As we discussed, we build unity by seeking to agree on essential items like the person of God, our need for the church, faith as the means of salvation, needing an entry point into a faith relationship, and the return of Christ. We won't always start off agreeing, but these issues hold enough importance that we need to strive for agreement on them. As we follow these guidelines, we'll live in the truth. I encourage you to commit yourself to a rigorous examination of what you believe and what others suggest. Seek truth that's consistent with God's Word. When you do, on the authority of God's true Word I promise you, "Then you will *know the truth,* and the truth *will set you free*" (John 8:32, emphasis added).

Freedom is a good thing. And that's the truth.

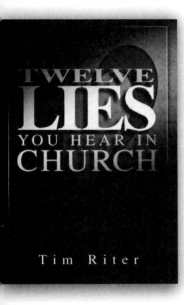

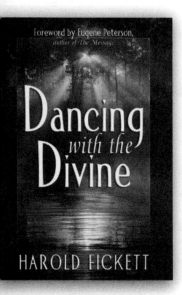

The Word at Work . . .

What would you do if you wanted to share God's love with children on the streets of your city? That's the dilemma David C. Cook faced in 1870s Chicago. His answer was to create literature that would capture children's hearts.

Out of those humble beginnings grew a worldwide ministry that has used literature to proclaim God's love and disciple generation after generation. Cook Communications Ministries is committed to personal discipleship—to helping people of all ages learn God's Word, embrace his salvation, walk in his ways, and minister in his name.

Opportunities—and Crisis

We live in a land of plenty—including plenty of Christian literature! But what about the rest of the world? Jesus commanded, "Go and make disciples of all nations" (Matt. 28:19) and we want to obey this commandment. But how does a publishing organization "go" into all the world?

There are five times as many Christians around the world as there are in North America. Christian workers in many of these countries have no more than a New Testament, or perhaps a single shared copy of the Bible, from which to learn and teach.

We are committed to sharing what God has given us with such Christians.

A vital part of Cook Communications Ministries is our international outreach, Cook Communications Ministries International (CCMI). Your purchase of this book, and of other books and Christian-growth products from Cook, enables CCMI to provide Bibles and Christian literature to people in more than 150 languages in 65 countries.

Cook Communications Ministries is a not-for-profit, self-supporting organization. Revenues from sales of our books, Bible curriculum, and other church and home products not only fund our U.S. ministry, but also fund our CCMI ministry around the world. One hundred percent of donations to CCMI go to our international literature programs.

...Around the World

CCMI reaches out internationally in three ways:

· Our premier International Christian Publishing Institute (ICPI) trains leaders from nationally led publishing houses around the world to develop evangelism and discipleship materials to transform lives in their countries.

· We provide literature for pastors, evangelists, and Christian workers in their national language. We provide study helps for pastors and lay leaders in many parts of the world, such as China, India, Cuba, Iran, and Vietnam.

· We reach people at risk—refugees, AIDS victims, street children, and famine victims—with God's Word. CCMI puts literature that shares the Good News into the hands of people at spiritual risk—people who might die before they hear the name of Jesus and are transformed by his love.

Word Power—God's Power

Faith Kidz, RiverOak, Honor, Life Journey, Victor, NexGen — every time you purchase a book produced by Cook Communications Ministries, you not only meet a vital personal need in your life or in the life of someone you love, but you're also a part of ministering to José in Colombia, Humberto in Chile, Gousa in India, or Lidiane in Brazil. You help make it possible for a pastor in China, a child in Peru, or a mother in West Africa to enjoy a life-changing book. And because you helped, children and adults around the world are learning God's Word and walking in his ways.

Thank you for your partnership in helping to disciple the world. May God bless you with the power of his Word in your life.

For more information about our international ministries, visit www.ccmi.org.